Issues in the Philosophy
of Language

ISSUES IN THE PHILOSOPHY OF LANGUAGE

Proceedings of the 1972 Oberlin Colloquium in Philosophy

Edited by
Alfred F. MacKay and Daniel D. Merrill

New Haven and London, Yale University Press, 1976

Copyright © 1976 by Yale University.

All rights reserved. This book may not be
reproduced, in whole or in part, in any
form (except by reviewers for the public
press), without written permission from the publishers.

Library of Congress catalog card number: 75-18178

International standard book number: 0-300-01828-2

Designed by Sally Sullivan
and set in I.B.M. Century Type
by Jay's Publishers Services, Inc., Scituate, Mass.,
and Printed in the United States of America by
The Alpine Press, Inc., South Braintree, Mass.

Published in Great Britain, Europe, and Africa by
Yale University Press, Ltd., London.
Distributed in Latin America by
Kaiman & Polon, Inc., New York City;
in Australasia by Book & Film Services,
Artarmon, N.S.W., Australia;
in Japan by John Weatherhill, Inc., Tokyo.

CONTENTS

PREFACE

This volume is the Proceedings of the thirteenth annual Oberlin Colloquium in Philosophy, held 14–16 April 1972. The colloquium is sponsored by the Department of Philosophy of Oberlin College to provide an opportunity for the presentation and discussion of new work. The 1972 colloquium consisted of six sessions, of which five were symposia. All of the papers are published here for the first time.

Each year the attempt is made to restrict the topics of the colloquium to a single general topic. For 1972, the topic was the philosophy of language, and the papers in this volume cover three central topics of current concern in that area: the relation between formal logic and the logic of natural languages; theories of belief and reference growing out of recent work in modal semantics; and the nature of speech acts and their expression.

In his opening paper, Alan Ross Anderson discusses the interplay between mathematically oriented methods of analysis and those derived from the study of ordinary language. He begins with Ryle's suggestion that the difference between formal and informal logic is like the difference between the military parade ground and the real battlefield. While sympathetic to this idea, Anderson argues that we must not be misled into believing that there is one parade ground that must be accepted on authority—that of Russell and Whitehead. The defense of a formal logic requires the use of that informal logic which we all share. He then discusses current disputes in the theory of entailment, after giving an example of a similar dispute in the history of physics. He criticizes traditional arguments which attempt to show that a contradiction implies any proposition by claiming that most uses of "or" are intensional, so that "p" does not entail "pVq." He concludes by reiterating that the philosophical interest of a formal logic lies not in its mathematical elegance but in whether it is a true theory of that which it is supposed to characterize.

Fred Sommers also discusses the relations between formal logic and natural language, but in a very different way. He points out that in traditional logic, the logical structure of a "regimented" sentence was one type of natural syntactic structure, but that this is not the case in the tradition deriving from Frege and

Russell. The traditional reason for using these new forms has been their greater power, but Sommers suggests that natural syntax is not as weak as modern logicians have supposed. Adopting a suggestion from Leibniz, Sommers then devises an algebraic notation for propositions such as "Socrates is wise." Using the positive and negative signs in several different ways, he then extends this notation to traditional categorical propositions, identity propositions, existence propositions, propositions with compound terms, compound propositions, and relational propositions. He regards his notation as a transcription of vernacular forms, rather than as a translation such as is provided in the Frege-Russell logic. Ontological problems are also avoided. Rules for syllogistic and immediate inference may then be stated, with the solving of ethymemes being a matter of solving an equation. Principles of identity are obtained and extensions of the system are suggested. He concludes that the gap between logical form and natural syntax may not be impossible to bridge, and that the representation of all logical signs by signs of opposition has an independent interest.

Saul Kripke's recent work on problems in the philosophy of language and metaphysics has inspired a great interest among philosophers. David Shwayder's paper arises from a symposium at the 1972 colloquium in which Kripke delivered a talk on "Vacuous Names and Mythical Kinds" and Shwayder served as commentator. In the absence of a version of Kripke's talk which could be included in this volume, Shwayder kindly consented to prepare an expanded version of his comments on Kripke's recent work. The result is a systematic interpretation and evaluation of Kripke's position, a position in which Shwayder finds much to endorse but also some sources of discomfort.

Shwayder begins by considering Kripke's views on necessity. He supports Kripke's distinction between questions of the *a prioricity* of knowledge and questions of the necessity of truths, as well as Kripke's recognition of the similarities between proper names of particulars and common names of natural kinds and stuffs. He finds similarities between Kripke's view that proper names are rigid designators and Arnauld's criticism of Leibniz's idea of an individual concept. From this view it follows that identity statements between names, when true, are necessarily true. However, Shwayder is concerned that Kripke seems also to hold that all identity statements, when true, are necessarily true. After raising the question of the necessity of identity, Shwayder goes on to examine Kripke's essentialism, and he finds problems in the fact that Kripke has added to traditional essential properties both the time and place of origin of a body as well as its material constitution. Shwayder also disputes Kripke's claim that there are properties involving modal operators, and he suggests that only truths, and not facts, can be said to be contingent or necessary.

Shwayder then turns to his second major topic, Kripke's treatment of the semantics of proper and common names. He first discusses proper names. He finds much to agree with in Kripke's view that proper names are rigid designators whose meanings are determined by a causal chain leading back to an act of naming, and whose referent can be fixed by a description which is not itself part of the meaning of the proper name, and he uses his own theory of proper names to illuminate Kripke's thesis that proper names are rigid designators. He compares Kripke's views on common names with those of Aristotle and Locke. While Kripke's views are similar to Locke's in some respects, he seems to differ from Locke in neglecting the distinction between substances and mixed modes. Shwayder finds important differences between identity statements concerning particulars and identity statements concerning sorts or stuffs, such as the statement that gold = element #79; and he disputes the thesis that these latter equations are even true. A basic distinction between substances and modes is that substances are fitted onto their instances whereas instances are fitted into modes; thus, substances must have "archetypes," while this is not true of modes. Natural kinds or substances cannot be defined in terms of any definite cluster of properties, but with modes the essence can be specified by "fiat." While substances and modes are thus distinct, the instances of substances must be fitted into modes in order to be scientifically fruitful. In this view it is possible that a substance and its corresponding modes are necessarily coextensive.

Shwayder concludes his analysis by considering briefly Kripke's views on fictions. He finds that Kripke's account of fictions blurs the distinction between names, such as those which occur in traditions, which are intended to have referents and fail to do so, and those "names" which occur in myths and stories which are not really names at all, but only pretended names. This provides a basis for disputing Kripke's claim that if Homer did not exist he could not have existed.

Robert Stalnaker provides a theory of propositions within the framework of a theory of possible worlds. He suggests that propositions be construed as functions from possible worlds into truth values. This accords with the common-sense notion that one understands a sentence when one understands the conditions under which it would be true or false. Stalnaker then argues for this account by placing it within the context of beliefs construed as functional states of a rational agent, and defined by their roles in determining the behavior of the agent. Such an account already contains the notion of alternative possible courses of events. It also suggests that two sentences express the same proposition if they are true in the same possible worlds. This definition has the advantage that it makes propositions independent of language. Stalnaker then considers possible difficulties with this theory. To those who have ontological worries over the existence of possible worlds, he replies that the fruitfulness of the theory gives us good reason to believe in the existence of such entities, in the absence of independent reasons for denying them. He considers more serious the fact that according to this theory, any two logically equivalent statements must express the same proposition, even though it is obvious that a person may believe one and disbelieve the other if he does not realize that they are equivalent. Rejecting several solutions to this problem, Stalnaker states that it should be resolved by noting that in such cases, the person really believes the proposition in question, but only fails to realize that it is expressed by a particular sentence. Since there are only two different propositions in mathematics—the necessarily true and the necessarily false—the objects of belief in mathematics are propositions asserting the relations between sentences and propositions. He uses a similar method to deal with our knowledge of identity statements.

Lawrence Powers begins his comments on Stalnaker's paper by objecting to Stalnaker's claim that fruitfulness alone is a sufficient ground for accepting the possible-worlds approach. The fruitfulness of a theory is not an adequate response to the objection that an entire approach is ludicrous; not the fruitfulness of a theory but its truth is the only question which matters. Powers denies that in talking about alternative situations or events in the usual sense we need be talking about alternative possible worlds in the sense of the proposed theory. Powers rejects Stalnaker's claims that logically equivalent propositions are identical and that whoever believes one believes the other. Rather than being functions from possible worlds to truth values, Powers suggests that propositions would be better construed as functions from desires to actions. Any attempt to define or individuate beliefs by their role in action must reject the condition that a person's beliefs are deductively closed. Powers concludes his comments by developing Piaget's idea that increased understanding of a proposition is reflected in readier interchange of equivalents and faster motion along chains of consequences, and by noting problems in attempting to individuate beliefs through their roles in actions.

Charles Landesman's paper is an attempt to take seriously the thesis that it is not words which refer, but that it is persons who refer, using words. The regularities of speech are human artifacts that acquire their function in the context of human action. This suggests that a difference which makes no difference in what people do or think is not a difference in what they mean or in what objects they mean or refer to. From this point of view, Landesman rejects the claim that there must always be a difference between referring and merely trying to refer. The nonexistence of the object does not mean that the speaker has failed to refer. Furthermore, referring need not be viewed as an act by which a speaker picks out or identifies an object for a hearer, since referring may occur in nonspoken acts of judgment. Descriptions of linguistic acts which apply to overt speech acts need not apply to covert acts of judgment. A related error is the claim that the existence of the object is needed not only for reference but also for the truth of statements, or at least for their truth or falsity. Other writers have attempted to avoid the counterintuitive results of this error by talking of fictional entities. Landesman denies that his view requires a nonstandard logic. The "existential" quantifier can be given an interpretation that is ontologically neutral, and an existence predicate can be introduced for existence assertions. In this view of reference, it is no longer reasonable to deny that predicates or even sentences may refer.

Jay Rosenberg believes that Landesman's "heretical" conclusions do not follow from his comparatively noncontroversial view of language. Since the consummation of many human activities depends upon conditions independent of human beliefs and intentions, Landesman must provide independent grounds for claiming that referring is not the type of action that is affected by such external factors. While Rosenberg accepts the intent of Landesman's claims that neither reference nor truth depend upon the existence of the object, he does so for different reasons: namely, because it is often the case that we do refer to things that do not exist. Not only are there fictional cases, but also incorrect references to existing objects. In referring to "the tallest building in my living room," it seems that I do fail to refer, and in such cases it is difficult to see how truth or falsity can apply. While Rosenberg accepts a noncommittal interpretation of the existential quantifier (with some qualifications), he suggests that Quine would say that it is not the quantifier itself, but certain uses of it to codify theories, that commits the user to the existence of certain entities. Rosenberg rejects Landesman's claim that linguistic acts of referring may be illuminated by nonlinguistic judgments. He believes that Landesman's account gives to mental images a function in judgment which has been convincingly refuted by Wittgenstein. Rosenberg concludes by asking whether reference is a relation between words and the world. If it is, it seems hard to see how a word such as "Pegasus" can be related to nothing at all. He sketches an account according to which reference is not a relation between words and the world, but in which the linguistic network as a whole is fitted to the world through nonsemantic real relations between items in the world and bits of language, extensionally conceived.

In his reply, Landesman is surprised that Rosenberg appears to agree with his main points, yet appears to say things inconsistent with them. He believes that his account of language has shown why reference is the type of activity that does not require an existing object for its successful completion. The fact that we apparently refer to nonexistent objects would not be accepted as evidence that we actually do so by anyone who held a theory of language that required the existence condition. It is not possible to determine the referent of a phrase such as "the tallest building in my living room" in the absence of context. He does agree, however, that in some cases truth and falsity do not apply. Landesman denies that he has used mental imagery in an objectionable way in his account of judgment. He claims in addition that, having dropped the existence condition, he can say that there is a relation between words that do exist and some things that do not exist. Rosenberg's account of sentences in the form "*W* refers to *X*" is, he claims, compatible with his own view that reference is a relation.

In his paper on "Illocutionary Suicide," Zeno Vendler deals with problems in the attempt to provide syntactical criteria for performative verbs, in the sense of J. L. Austin. He points out that there are many verbs of saying, such as "allege," "goad," and "scold," that do not satisfy the Austinian mark of occurring in the first person present tense. The purpose of his paper is to explain why such quasi-performatives lack this characteristic mark of performatives, by explaining what goes wrong when these verbs are used in a performative way. To say "I allege that p" is to ask you to take my word for p while adding that it is unworthy of belief. Vendler defines the illocutionary aim of a speech act as the mental act or mental state which the speaker intends the hearer to adopt. If a speaker uses an explicit performative, he must select a performative which expresses the same illocutionary aim, without at the same time having a feature (a "spoiling factor") which undermines that aim. Vendler then applies this to other quasi-performatives, such as "insinuate," "incite," "scold," and "scoff." He suggests that while Austin took the first person present tense use of illocutionary verbs as primary, we should take the third person use as primary. Furthermore, we recognize that in most cases the performative use of these verbs would not frustrate the illocutionary aim of the speaker, but that in some cases it will through the existence of a spoiling factor. Moore's Paradox and the Liar's Paradox are then discussed in these terms.

Charles Caton begins his comments by discussing problems in the formulation of Austin's mark—that performative verbs characteristically occur in the first person singular present indicative active form. He then agrees that Vendler has located a problem in Austin's account, but wonders just what the problem is. Vendler's examples are verbs of saying that are not genuine performative verbs. Austin's thesis is that "to perform a locutionary act is in general . . . also and *eo ipso* to perform an illocutionary act," and this is not undermined as long as there is some other illocutionary verb for each quasi-performative verb of saying. Caton then examines the details of usage which Vendler cites for "allege" and "brag," and claims that these details are incorrect. For instance, "allege" does not suggest the falsity of what is put forward, only that it is done so without proof. Caton closes his comments by citing examples of other quasi-performative verbs which cannot be accounted for in terms of illocutionary aim, and by considering certain devices that convert to a near-performative use many verbs that do not have performative first person uses. He also notes that verbs of manner of saying cannot have their nonperformativeness explained by Vendler's theory.

The authors of the papers included in this volume come from eight universities: Anderson from the University of Pittsburgh, Sommers from Brandeis University, Shwayder and Caton from University of Illinois, Stalnaker from Cornell University, Powers

from Wayne State University, Vendler from the University of
California, San Diego, Landesman from Hunter College of the
City University of New York, and Rosenberg from the University
of North Carolina at Chapel Hill. The members of the Department of Philosophy of Oberlin College are indebted to the
speakers for their contributions and to the other philosophers
who attended for their participation. They also wish to thank
Oberlin College for its continuing support of the Oberlin
Philosophy Colloquium.

LOGIC AND SHOULDER-SHRUGGING

Alan Ross Anderson

My intent in this paper is to make some remarks, not alto-gether original or conclusive, about two strains in the contem-porary philosophical tradition which go in tandem, uneasily, under the heading of "analytic philosophy." Analytic philosophy has of course been with us since Socrates began to ask crucial questions about "what we mean when we say . . . ." Anyone familiar with the Platonic corpus can come up with countless examples: *what do we mean* by "piety," "virtue," "friendship," "justice," and so on?

There are also philosophers of another persuasion, European continental rather than local, who try to explain to us what life is really like, in one way or another, and for some reason this kind of philosophizing is put in the synthetic camp. At least one of these philosophers in the Continental tradition believes that first we should take things apart (analysis), and *then* we should put them back together again (synthesis).

Though I am inclined to suspect the spatial metaphor just used, I feel that most philosophers worth their salt are involved in both enterprises. Certainly Plato and Aristotle had both analytic and synthetic interests, and it is hard to find significant figures in philosophy since their time who did not have both. I find it difficult, at any rate, to locate among the philosophers we think of as "major" (in the sense that we are willing to condemn our students to study their writings) any who fail to have a penchant for both the analytic and synthetic branches of the topic.

The foregoing is simply prefatory to the remark that I have been asked to say something about the "philosophy of lan-guage," and since I take it that this topic belongs on the analy-tic branch of the philosophical tree, I will accordingly disqualify myself from making recommendations about life, reality, and how we ought to conduct ourselves.

The two "strains" in the analytic tradition I mentioned at the outset are reflected in the attitudes and methods of those of us who pretend that we are mathematicians and those of us who pretend that we are sociologists. What ties these two groups together is the notion of "conceptual analysis," that is, trying

1

to figure out in a clear way what we are talking about. Any reflective chap is willing to admit that he sometimes does not know what he is talking about. We get *confused*, and just do not know what to say. So we try to straighten things out, and trying to analyze our confusion leads to the two tendencies or strains mentioned above.

We might try to do things on the Euclidean model, as mathematical logicians in the Boole–Frege–Whitehead–Russell tradition tend to do. The spectacular success of this mathematical approach to "conceptual analysis" of such notions as sets, or numbers, or lines and planes, or some aspects of formal logic makes this option look very attractive.

We might on the other hand try to do things on a sociological model, as Austin and the New Testament Wittgenstein did. The analytic question becomes "What are *we* (as a community) *doing* with the language we share?" To this analytic strain belongs talk about "the logic of imperatives," "the logic of action verbs," and since this kind of talk has to do with how we communicate with each other, it might as well include "the logic of shoulder-shrugging," or "the logic of eyebrow-lifting," and the like.

To recapitulate, we have two vocabularies: "⊃," "&," "∼," "⊢," "→," " ∃x," "∀x," etc., all very aseptic, and "category-mistake," "locutionary," "illocutionary," "perlocutionary," "noustic," "phrastic," "following a rule," etc., all of which are equally technical, but subject to the constraints of vagueness which are built into the language in which they are couched, namely, "ordinary" English.

The first has to do with the mathematical analysis, the second with the sociological analysis. I will discuss in the remainder of this paper the interplay between these two ways of doing "linguistic" or "conceptual" analysis. (It was Wilfrid Sellars, incidentally, who first mentioned to me that from both points of view, "strictly speaking" and "strictly thinking" come to pretty much the same thing.)

To help locate the topic I want to discuss, I refer to the last of Gilbert Ryle's Tarner Lectures, entitled "Formal and Informal Logic," published in his 1953 volume, *Dilemmas.* I am on the whole sympathetic with the picture he draws there, but I would like to offer a somewhat different sketch of what is going on in the differences of attitude, opinion, or interests between those who prefer mathematical metaphors in logic and those who prefer sociological ones.

One of Ryle's interesting and illuminating parallels between "formal" and "informal" logic compares the former to the military parade ground and the latter to the real battlefield. Parade ground drill certainly teaches us something, though it is hard to say what; but whatever it is, it is *not* the quick wit that is required to be successful in guerilla warfare. Formal logic is, as I understand Ryle, done on a Euclidean plane in lockstep; informal logic requires the ability to use a contour map, and to keep a sharp eye out for unsuspected hazards. My own point, which I will introduce with another parallel or metaphor, is simply this: that we can be misled into the belief that there *is* a paradeground that we must accept on authority, and that since the authorities have provided us with such beautiful products as *Principia Mathematica* (*PM*), or Hilton Hotels, it is not our business (as philosophers) to ask questions about the language of *PM*, or about the lounge in the hotel.

The way most of us are taught formal logic leads us to believe that systems of formal logic are languages to be used. Indeed, Russell and Old Testament Wittgenstein encouraged the idea, as did Carnap, in calling systems of mathematical logic "languages." And this leads to the contra-Rylean metaphor I had in mind.

It is said that during the depths of the 1929–1932 depression in the United States, there was a man who owned a warehouse-ful of candles, which he was unable to sell at a profit—or even at a loss. So he decided in desperation to sell them to retailers, in the hope of getting *something* out of the enterprise. He did this with some success, but then began to get complaints from the retailers that housewives had been bringing the candles back, and complaining that the candles had no wicks. A check at the warehouse revealed that in all probability *none* of the candles had wicks, so the owner began to trace the series of transactions back to the manufacturer. There were some twenty or more transactions between the manufacture in 1922 and the attempted disposal of the candles in 1932. And when the manufacturer was finally located, he explained, "The candles didn't *need* wicks; they weren't *intended* for burning, they were simply meant for buying and selling, as the market went up or down."

I think that there is a moral here for the distinction between formal "languages" and informal ones. The formal "languages" are not intended to be used; they are intended to be *talked about.* No logician has ever walked into a classroom and said, "p." (Followed perhaps by a student saying, "p horseshoe pVq," whereupon the instructor says, "Omigod, pVq!" and then collapses in a faint.)

What we do of course is to talk *about* these formal "languages," but in what language do we speak? Well, in whatever "natural language," or "informal logic," we have in common. This is what Haskell Curry has frequently called the "U-language," or "Universal language": the one we (as a sociological community) happen to speak (or, in difficult cases, have enough linguistically in common so that we can communicate).

What does this do to Ryle's lock-step analogy? Not much, but something. He locates lock-step with *the* parade ground, and "informal logic" with the battlefield. I want to agree with this, but relax the idea that there is *one* parade ground. In particular, I want to claim that Ryle's (apparent) view that there is only one parade ground (the official one) is wrong, and that one *real* and important informal logical battle has to do with where parade grounds are. What is philosophically interesting about mathematics and mathematical logic is *not* that there are a lot of mathematical truths ("formal logic") to which we are in some way obliged to give allegiance (as Frege, Russell, and Old Testament Wittgenstein would have us believe), but rather that orthodox as well as unorthodox formal logics require philosophical defense—a defense which can be couched only in the terms of the informal "logic" we all share—or share to some reasonable extent, at least.

The tradition in this particular sort of argle-bargle demands that we concentrate on an example or two, and I have a couple in hand.

The first has to do with physics, and for the information on the history of the problem I want to talk about, I am indebted almost entirely to a fascinating article by L. L. Laudan on the *vis viva* controversy.[1] The controversy, which came out of the writings of Leibniz, had to do with the measurement of force. Monads, we recall, were *materia prima*, and as such had a primitive active force (entelechy), combined with a primitive passive force (matter); the two were indissolubly linked. *Materia secunda* results from combinations of monads, where impenetrability, extension, inertia, momentum, and the like are accounted for by the passive force of the monads themselves; but there is also an active force derived from the association of monads, a *vis viva*. All this is very obscure, and I do not want to try to elucidate it here—I do not know how to. But in the early eighteenth century there was a vigorous philosophical controversy concerning the measurement of the *vis viva*, the *active force* deriving from a combination of monads.

---

1. "The *vis viva* Controversy, a Post Mortem," *Isis* 59 (1968): 131–43.

I have not seen the problem put exactly in the following way by early eighteenth-century natural philosophers (as physicists are still sometimes called in official circles in Cambridge University). At any rate, here is a guess as to what the controversy was about.

If someone drops a pebble on my head from a distance of two inches, it does not hurt very much, but if it is dropped from a distance of about twelve feet, it hurts noticeably. What is the "active force" of the impact involved? Or, somewhat more accurately, how can we *measure* the intuitive idea involved? Debate raged. Kantians held that the *vis viva* was best measured by mass times velocity (mv, a notion we now call *momentum*); Leibnitzians on the other hand claimed that force should be measured by mv^2. So on the one hand we have an intuitive idea ("how much does it hurt?"), and on the other, a notion from physics, or physics-cum-psychology ("how can we *measure* how much it hurts?").

The debate about this question had a solution of sorts, which (as Laudan remarks) was put forth in d'Alembert's *Traité de dynamique* of 1743; d'Alembert said in the introduction roughly that the whole controversy was simply "a matter of words," and that nothing more need be said about it. Much more *was* said about it, as Laudan points out, but certainly our current ways of speaking allow us to say with authority in elementary physics classes that momentum = mv, and force = ma.

(Laudan points out amusingly that though there is a tradition among historians of science that d'Alembert *solved* the problem in 1743, discussion of the difficulty persisted for many years after, and that presumably the source of the idea that d'Alembert solved the problem is an article on the subject in the *Encyclopédie*, the article being written by . . . I'll let you guess. Yes, you guessed correctly.)

Now what does all this mean? Simply, as it seems to me, that there was a lot of philosophical (analytic informal logical) argument about some mathematics (formal logic), which was *presented as if* it had a certain intuitive significance. What intuitive significance it had was a subject for informal debate. *Where* was the parade ground—mv or ma (or perhaps mv^2)?

The moral I wish to draw is that the entertaining informal logical arguments have to do with *locating* the parade ground, rather than assuming that we already know where it is and then (as Ryle says) coming to believe "the scenario-writer who represents fighting soldiers as heroes going berserk in close columns of platoons."

There is another example, somewhat closer to my heart than the historical example concerning the *vis viva*. Nuel Belnap and I, building on the work of Wilhelm Ackermann, Alonzo Church, and Moh Shaw-Kwei (though none of them is to be blamed for such errors as we have made of their work), have argued as vigorously as we could that the entire pre-1956 community of mathematical analysts of linguistic matters connected with logic were simply and flatly in error on a crucial point: namely, what we should mean by "if— then—."

This second example has to do with the notion of "entailment," as introduced by G. E. Moore, who wanted the word to mean "the converse of deducibility." That is, we will say that *A* entails *B* just in case *B* is deducible from *A*. As everyone knows, there has developed an enormous literature about the notion, much of it centering around a family of arguments leading to such conclusions as that "a contradiction entails every proposition," or "any proposition entails a necessary proposition." So we are asked to believe things like these:

$$(p\&\sim p) \mathrel{\rightarrow\mkern-9mu{\scriptscriptstyle 3}} q, \text{ and}$$
$$p \mathrel{\rightarrow\mkern-9mu{\scriptscriptstyle 3}} (q \lor \sim q),$$

where the hook is that of some system of strict implication.

The mathematical types tend to say, "Well, sorry about that, but it just happens that our correct intuitions about truth-functions and modality lead inevitably to these unexpected results, so we simply have to swallow them," and the sociological types tend to say, "But look here, *no one* uses the language like that, unless they've been conned by the mathematical types into thinking that the hook may be read 'if—then——'; all you have to do is read Austin on *Ifs and Cans*, and you'll be disabused of all this nonsense."

There must be something to be said on both sides, or else there wouldn't have been so much said on both sides. And in order to elucidate what I think is to be said about both sides, I will use an illustration from a paper by E. M. Curley,[2] who considers one of the Lewis paradoxes as follows:

> We cannot deny that an impossible proposition strictly implies (i.e. entails) any proposition whatever without sacrificing one of the following logical laws:
> (1)   A&B entails A
> (2)   A&B entails B

2. "Lewis and Entailment," *Philosophical Studies* 23 (1972): 198-204.

(3) A entails A∨B
(4) A∨B and ∼ A entail B.

For given these laws, it is a simple matter to derive any proposition whatever from a representative impossible proposition. E.g.,

(a) A&∼A   premise
(b) A   from (a), by (1)
(c) A∨B   from (b), by (3)
(d) ∼A   from (a), by (2)
(e) B   from (c) and (d), by (4).

Lewis regarded this pattern of argument as providing independent grounds for thinking that impossible propositions do entail any proposition whatever.

Now the only objection I have to this passage is the parenthetical remark "(i.e. entails)" in the first sentence; it would be hard to find a clearer example of a *petitio principii*, since the question involved is whether or not strict implication *is* a reconstruction of Moore's idea of logical consequence, or its converse, entailment. Of course this is not a charge against Curley—he makes it perfectly clear that the *petitio* involved was invented by C. I. Lewis, and maintained by those who followed him. And Curley goes on with equal fairness to paraphrase an argument put forth by Belnap and myself, to the effect that the Lewis tribe was in error. As he correctly says:

Lewis claims (i) that 'A entails B' means that B is deducible from A by 'some mode of inference which is valid' and (ii) that there is a valid mode of inference from A&∼A to B. We accept (i) and deny (ii), Lewis's argument is not valid, because it employs 'A∨B and ∼ A entail B'. This principle, of course, is valid in one sense, viz. it is impossible for the premises to be true and the conclusion false. But if Lewis is presupposing that criterion of validity, then he is begging the question. For that criterion of validity would commit us directly to the paradoxes without any need for Lewis's argument.

If Lewis tries to escape the charge of question-begging by maintaining that 'A∨B and ∼ A entail B' and the other principles he uses are valid in the sense of having always been accepted and used without question, then we deny that this is the case. No one has ever accepted or used 'A∨B and ∼ A entail B' except a logician making jokes. That principle, which is invalid, needs to be distinguished from 'A⊻B and ∼ A entail B' [where the boxed wedge represents some form of *inten-*

sional disjunction], which is valid and is the principle actually being used whenever anyone outside a logic classroom produces a disjunctive syllogism. Lewis cannot claim to be using 'A☑B and ~ A entails B' in this argument unless he also employs 'A entails A☑B' in going from (b) to (c). But that principle would clearly be invalid.

This seems to me to be a fair summary of what Belnap and I have said, and I do not mean to tax Curley for having misunderstood us, or for having perversely put our position in a bad light. In fact he goes on to present some penetrating criticisms of a passage which *seems*, as he says, to present the view that "the intensional use of 'or' has something to do with the support of conditional statements." He goes on to quote a passage from the same article by Belnap and myself:

> When one says "that is either *Drosophila melonogaster* or *D. virilis*, I'm not sure which," and on finding that it wasn't *D. melonogaster*, concludes that it was *D. virilis*, no fallacy is being committed. But this is precisely because "or" in this context *means* "if it isn't one, then it is the other." Of course, there is no question here of a relation of logical entailment . . . evidently some other sense of "if . . . then—" is involved. But it should be equally clear that it is not simply the truth-functional "or" either, from the fact that a speaker would naturally feel that if what he said was true, then if it hadn't been *D. virilis*, it *would* have been *D. melonogaster*.

In the paper in question, Belnap and I issued a challenge to someone other than a logician making jokes to find a serious example of an "if— then—" proposition which is related to the *truth-functional* "or" in the way we have been classically led to believe. (We added that if no such examples exist, then we will feel we have made our case, and if examples do exist, then we reserve the right to try to find something funny about them.)

This challenge was met by Curley, who was to a certain extent defending C. I. Lewis. He asks us to consider the following, which, he says, looks like an "unequivocal counterexample":

A: "Who said: 'Give me liberty or give me death'?"
B: "It was either Nathan Hale or Patrick Henry—I'm not sure which."
C: "It wasn't Nathan Hale. *He* said: 'I only regret that I have but one life to give for my country'."
A: "Then I guess it must have been Patrick Henry."

Curley goes on to say:

> I think it clear that B will take his disjunctive statement to
> be confirmed if he later learns that it was Patrick Henry; that
> he would have accepted 'If it wasn't Nathan Hale, then it was
> Patrick Henry' as a paraphrase of that disjunctive statement;
> and that he would find faintly absurd the suggestion that he
> should be prepared to assent to "If Patrick Henry hadn't said
> 'Give me liberty or give me death', Nathan Hale would have."

I agree in part, in the sense that the original Anderson–Belnap
claim was too strong, but exercising the right to find something
funny about the example reserved above, I contend that there *is*
a subjunctive conditional which in some sense "follows from"
B's disjunction—namely, "If 'Patrick Henry' had not been the
correct answer to A's question, then 'Nathan Hale' would have
been." So *some* subjunctive conditional seems to follow, as
required, though not the one we suggested originally. But this
seems to me a weak line of defense.

A stronger line is this: I have doubts about whether B would
"take his disjunctive statement to be confirmed if he later learns
that it was Patrick Henry" (something funny again). For suppose
that the conversation goes on with

D: "It *was* Patrick Henry; I just looked it up in Bartlett."

It would seem again "faintly absurd" if we were to hear:

B: "Aha! I was right all along."

And we might well imagine a fifth party to the conversation
chiming in with

E: "But didn't you hear what D *said*? What he said confirmed
A's second remark, not yours."

But we repeat that such questions are moot ("or," after all,
sometimes means "that is to say"), and that we have no general
theory of intensional senses of the word which satisfies even us,
let alone others. Our claim is simply that in ordinary English
"or" is rarely, if ever, used truth-functionally; just as "if— then—"
is rarely, if ever, used truth-functionally or intuitionistically; so
rarely, indeed, that we don't know of a single *unequivocal*
counterexample to the claim that natural, serious uses of "or"
as a propositional connective *always* can be used to support a
counterfactual conditional.

I would like to summarize at this point. The argument I have been pursuing runs like this. If we believe with Ryle that *there is one* classically defined parade ground on which we are (somehow) obliged to march when doing mathematics, or formal logic, or geometry, and if we also believe that informal "logic" has to do with the sociological commentary on how we use a natural language, then we get a very different picture from that seen from the *inside* of those of us who pretend to be mathematicians. From the latter standpoint, the picture looks more like the construction of a bridge, or rather the designing of one. When one is presented with the blueprints, it is obviously fair to ask whether the design will in fact do what it was intended to do—and it seems to me that *that* is just where the difference between formal and informal logic lies.

Someone proposes a theory with a mathematical or "formal" flavor; what we then do is discuss whether it is a *good* mathematical theory of what it is *supposed* to be a theory of. That is where the philosophical interest of mathematics and formal logic lies. But that is nothing new. What is philosophically interesting in formal logic—or mathematics, or the natural or behavioral sciences, or philosophy—is whether or not some view of the matter is true (or with a concession to the pragmatists, the *best* view).

Postscript.   In the paper presented above, I have attempted to adopt a rather even-tempered tone, out of deference, I suppose, to the polite and well-behaved audience to whom it was read. But it would be misleading to the reader if he were left with the impression that my real sentiments are as cool as those expressed here. The fact of the matter is that I believe that what Ryle believes, in the Frege–Russell tradition, is *the* formal parade ground exists only in Cloud-cuckooland, and is composed of terrain on which, learned authorities to the contrary notwithstanding, *no man ever trod.* Anyone interested in seeing me in my true colors on the topic is invited to read my article "An intensional interpretation of truth-values,"[3] or the book *Entailment*[4] by Belnap and myself.

3. *Mind* 81 (1972): 348–71.
4. Alan Ross Anderson and Nuel Belnap, *Entailment,* vol. 1 (Princeton: Princeton University Press, 1975).

LOGICAL SYNTAX IN NATURAL LANGUAGE

Fred Sommers

The syntax of modern logic is specified by the formation-rules for an artificial language.[1] It was developed in conscious opposition to the traditional logic of terms, the so-called subject-predicate logic whose syntactic model was the grammatical structure of declarative sentences of natural languages.

The difference between the traditional and the modern approach to logical syntax is clear from common examples. Even the traditional logician regimented his sentences for purposes of logical reckoning. Thus, a sentence like 'every sparrow chirps' is amended by him to 'every sparrow is a chirper', a transformation that ensures grammatical interchangeability of the terms in subject and predicate positions that permits inference to, say, 'every non-chirper is a non-sparrow'. For similar reasons, a sentence of the form 'only *A* is *B*' would be dealt with in the form 'no non-*A* is *B*'. The sort of regimentation practiced by the traditional logician is syntactically innocuous; in the regimented sentence there is no shift to new syntactical devices; the basic subject-predicate structure of the original sentence has not been disturbed. It is fair to say that the premodern logicians did not really distinguish between the logical structure of a regimented sentence and its natural syntactical structure. This is as true of Leibniz as it is true of Aristotle. Both logicians assumed implicitly that logical form coincided with certain elementary standard grammatical structures in natural languages. Indeed, Leibniz was convinced that a felicitous notation for the natural syntax of the sentence must inevitably provide us with a useful instrument for logical reckoning.

1. See also by the same author: "On a Fregean Dogma," *Problems in the Philosophy of Mathematics* (Amsterdam: North Holland Publishing Co., 1967), pp. 47–81; "Do We Need Identity?", *Journal of Philosophy* 66 (1969): 499–504; "On Concepts of Truth in Natural Languages," *Review of Metaphysics* 23 (1969): 259–86; "The Logical and the Extra-Logical," *Boston Studies in the Philosophy of Science* 14 (1973), ed. Cohen and Wartofsky, pp. 235–51; "The Calculus of Terms," *Mind* 79 (1970): 1–40; "Existence and Predication," in *Logic and Ontology*, ed. M. Munitz (New York: New York University Press, 1973), pp. 159–74; "Distribution Matters," *Mind* 333 (January 1975): 27–46.

Frege and Russell opposed this Leibnizian ideal, believing it to be a poor research program. Russell thought that Leibniz's respect for natural syntax was the principal cause of his failure to devise an adequate logical calculus. And, indeed, the modern idea of logical form contrasts very sharply with the assumption that logical syntax coincides with the syntax of any natural language. One may even say that the analytical technique of modern quantification theory ensures the failure of Leibniz's program. Frege saw his own logical syntax as a *Zerfällung*, a decomposition of the subject-predicate structure of natural syntax in favor of a structure of function and argument. And if one takes Fregean syntax as canonical, then one is also sympathetic to warnings about the intrinsically misleading nature of the grammatical structures of sentences of natural language. Most of us have been brought up to suspect the syntax of natural language as deceptive and superficial; in the twentieth century such suspicion is the mark of a critical philosopher, and it has lately provided inspiration to linguists as well.

The contemporary logician radically transforms 'every sparrow chirps', rendering it as 'everything is such that it chirps or is not a sparrow'. The syntactical gap between canonical form and vernacular form is wide; the two sentences belong to different languages, one natural and logically imperfect, the other artificial and logically perspicuous and powerful. In recognition of the gap, logicians properly speak of the canonical formula as a "translation" of the natural sentence. The rules of such "translation" are very imperfectly understood; even its meaning is not clear. The linguistic problems posed by the adoption of a technical and artificial syntax for logic are only just beginning to be taken seriously. For the present we take note of the fact that the canonical idioms of the artificial syntax are only remotely and problematically related to the syntax of the vernacular originals.

Why have philosophers and logicians accepted and "canonized" an artificial syntax that is so radically at variance with the surface syntax of declarative sentences of natural language? The answer is familiar enough. Logical syntax is first of all the syntax of a language that has an adequate degree of inference power. And while it is true that the older subject-predicate logic has the virtue of syntactic naturalness, it is just as true that the Leibnizian program has not come up with anything that could rival modern predicate logic as a compre-

hensive instrument for logical reckoning. A logical syntax as
natural as it is powerful is a nice thing if you can get it. If
philosophers have abandoned it they did so with understandable reluctance. But abandonment was indicated. Between an
adequate logic, however artificial, and an inadequate logic,
however natural, the right choice is clear, and clearheaded
philosophers have made it.

If any question still remains, it is whether natural syntax is
really as inferior for logical purposes as modern logicians have
judged it to be. In this connection it is customary to point to
Leibniz's inability to formalize relational inferences and to his
failure to provide for arguments that require such simple
principles as existential generalization or universal instantiation. These and other inadequacies of a logic whose syntax is
natural are familiar. Nevertheless, a doubt may legitimately
persist. The Leibnizian program has failed—so far. But no one
has ever shown it to be unrealizable in principle. Is natural
syntax logically inadequate? In raising this question I wish to
do more than raise the ghost of traditional logic for still
another shuffle in the attic of discarded logical doctrines of
yesteryear. I think I can show that Leibniz's program has
better than a ghost of a chance to be successfully realized. I
think that Leibniz was right—and right in an interesting way.

Let me say what I mean by his being interestingly right. It
has recently been proposed that logical form, in the guise of
canonical structures of modern predicate logic, coincides with
natural syntax at the level of the deep structures of empirical
grammars. I find such proposals uninteresting. Positing structures is one thing. But no one seriously pretends that a suitable scratching of the natural surface actually reveals the syntax of Frege's logic. Of course one supplies transformations
to the surface. But so far the controls on admissible transformations have not been well specified and the postulation
of deep structures along with suitable transformations is
altogether too easy for talk of empirical discoveries. It goes
without saying that no structures postulated at the level of
deep structure need in any way appear intuitively natural, and
so even this control is lacking. Any empirical claim that the
artificial syntactical devices of predicate logic are to be found
alive and natural in the deep structure must be viewed with
suspicion.

For Leibniz, the coincidence of logic and language is
assumed at the level of the surface structure of regimented

sentences. Now the thesis that logical and linguistic structures coincide at the surface is interesting. It is not speculative, not postulational, and any specific suggestion along these lines is easy to test. I have said that Leibniz—and Aristotle—were right in their implicit belief in a logical structure in natural language. I shall now begin to show what has led me to this reactionary persuasion.

Leibniz made many attempts to devise a logical grammar for categorical propositions in a manner that would facilitate the mechanical reckoning of valid arguments. One suggestion, unfortunately isolated and undeveloped, is found in his youthful work, *De Arte Combinatoria*.

> Thomas Hobbes . . . rightly stated that everything done by the mind is a *computation* by which is understood the addition of a sum or the subtraction of a difference. So just as there are two primary signs of algebra and analytics, + and -, in the same way there are as it were two copulas, 'is' and 'is not; in the former case the mind compounds, in the latter it divides.[2]

Following this suggestion of Leibniz's we shall represent the proposition 'Socrates is wise' as the algebraic expression '$S + W$'; the proposition 'Socrates isn't wise' is correspondingly represented as '$S - W$'. In the same algorithmic spirit we shall represent negative words and particles like 'not', 'no', and 'un-' as minus signs. This enables us to express some familiar logical relations algebraically:

$S + W = S - (-W)$ Socrates is wise = Socrates isn't unwise

$S - W = S + (-W)$ Socrates isn't wise = Socrates is unwise

'Wise' and 'unwise' exhaust a range; such terms are logical contraries. We are representing 'unwise' as '$-W$'; analogously we could represent 'wise' by '$+W$'. In natural language a positive prefix is not available. But even in arithmetic the positive sign is usually suppressed for reasons of notational economy. We could use '+7' for the positive number but this would be wasteful; the distinction between positive and negative numbers is sufficiently marked by the overt use of a *single* sign. In effect, the absence of the negative sign in '7' is an implicit positive sign.

2. G. H. Parkinson, ed. and trans., *Leibniz Logical Papers* (Oxford: Clarendon Press, 1966), p. 3.

Notational economy thus dictates the suppression of positive signs. But this ought not obscure the fact that the terms of traditional logic are understood to be "charged" positively or negatively. The choice of charge may be arbitrary. Thus 'wet' and 'dry' are logical contraries. If we consider 'wet' to be positive we will represent 'dry' as '$-w$'; if 'dry' is our choice for the positive term, 'wet' becomes '$-d$'. So viewed, each term is syntactically complex; it consists of a positive or negative sign and a lexical element. In older parlance, the term consists of a syncategorematic and an autocategorematic element. This complexity is made notationally explicit when we represent logical contraries with both signs of opposition, writing '$+W$' for 'wise' and '$-W$' for 'unwise'. Although we shall in the main omit positive signs, we shall often represent positive terms with explicit positive signs.

In the algebraic notation for logical syntax, the word 'is' (and other variants of the positive copula) is *plus* and the word 'not' (and other negative particles) is *minus.* We shall call a proposition that uses these logical signs and no others a *primitive predication.* Examples of primitive predications are 'creatures were stirring' and 'no creatures were stirring'. The only logical elements in these propositions are 'no' and 'were'.

It is obvious that primitive predications can be represented as algebraic expressions. For example, the form 'no x is y' or 'not an x is a y' is primitive. It is represented by the following expression:

$$-(x + y).$$

The contradictory form 'an x is a y' is represented as

$$x + y.$$

To make the opposition between contradictory predications notationally explicit we will often prefix '$x + y$' by a plus sign:

$$-(x + y) \qquad \text{not an x is a y}$$

$$+(x + y) \qquad \text{"yes" an x is a y.}$$

If all suppressed positive signs are made explicit the two primitive forms of predication are represented thus:

$$-[(+x) + (+y)]$$

$$+[(+x) + (+y)].$$

Note that in the positive form, the plus sign plays several different semantic roles. In its left-most occurrence it is a sign of affirmation. In the two occurrences to the immediate left of '*x*' and '*y*' it is a sign of positive term quality. The third plus sign represents 'is', the positive copula. The place of the sign determines its semantic role. The general form of primitive predications will include all possible combinations of positive or negative assertions and positive or negative copulas. The omnibus form is

$$\pm[(\pm x) \pm (\pm y)].$$

The first sign of a primitive predication indicates whether it has positive or negative quality. We shall speak of positive and negative "valence." A predication of positive valence has the form +[....]; a predication of negative valence has the form −[....]. Predications that differ in valence will be called heterogeneous; predications of like valence will be called homogeneous or *convalent.* An equation between two predications that are convalent will be called homogeneous. If the sides of the equation are heterogeneous, the equation will be called heterogeneous.

The algebraic representation is logically effective. The following general principle governs logical equivalence between primitive predications:

E Primitive predications are logically equivalent if and only if they are equal and convalent.

Using *E* we can establish the equivalence of 'no *x* is un-*y*' and 'no un-*y* is *x*' by examining the equation '−[(+*x*) + (−*y*)] = −[(−*y*) + (+*x*)] '. The equation is homogeneous and it is algebraically correct. Therefore its sides are logically equivalent.

We are developing Leibniz's algorithmic suggestion in the direction of a more comprehensive logical syntax for natural language. We have yet to show how to use the algorithm for sentences containing logical words other than 'is' and 'not'. To do this we first consider a schedule of four primitive propositions. This schedule is equivalent to a schedule of the four general categoricals usually found in traditional textbooks, it contains only such signs as can be given a plus-minus representation:

Explicit Transcription	*Original*	*Direct Transcription*
−[(+x) + (−y)]	No x is an un-y	−[x + (−y)]
−[(+x) + (+y)]	No x is a y	−(x + y)

Explicit Transcription	*Original*	*Direct Transcription*
+[(+x) + (+y)]	An x is a y	x + y
+[(+x) + (−y)]	An x is an un-y	x + (−y)

The primitive predictions of this schedule are equivalent to a standard A, E, I, O schedule containing words of quantity like 'every' and 'some'. This suggests that we can use primitive predications to define these words in terms of the primitive signs 'is' and 'not'. Using the primitive predications we can derive new forms of proposition with new logical elements. The definitions of 'every' and 'some' are implicit in the following equivalences:

1. every x is y   = not an x is not-y

2. every x is not-y   = not an x is a y

3. some x is y   = not every x is not-y

4. some x is not-y   = not every x is y

The definitions of 'some' in 3 and 4 are based on the prior definitions of 'every' in 1 and 2. But direct definitions may be given:

5. some x is y   = an x is a y

6. some x is not-y   = an x is a not-y.

By definition, any predication beginning with 'every' is negative in valence; any predication beginning with 'some' is positive in valence. This suggests that 'every' is a negative sign while 'some' is positive. And indeed, if we represent 'every' by a minus sign and 'some' by a plus sign, all the definitional equivalences become true algebraic equations:

$$1. \ +[-(+x) + (+y)] \ = \ -[(+x) + (-y)]$$
$$2. \ +[-(+x) + (-y)] \ = \ -[(+x) + (+y)]$$
$$3. \ +[+(+x) + (+y)] \ = \ -[-(+x) + (-y)]$$
$$4. \ +[+(+x) + (-y)] \ = \ -[-(+x) + (+y)]$$
$$5. \ +[+(+x) + (+y)] \ = \ +[(+x) + (+y)]$$
$$6. \ +[+(+x) + (-y)] \ = \ +[(+x) + (-y)]$$

In the algebraic syntax for traditional logic, the difference between universal and particular quantity is seen as an opposition of negative and positive valence. We now extend the syntactic

characterization of valence to include the nonprimitive categorical predications.

A positive or particular categorical proposition has either the
form $+[+(\pm x) \pm (\pm y)]$ or the form $-[-(\pm x) \pm (\pm y)]$. A negative
or universal categorical has either the form $-[+(\pm x) \pm (\pm y)]$ or
the form $+[-(\pm x) \pm (\pm y)]$. In other words, particular quantity is
positive valence, universal quantity is negative valence.

Any algebraic transformation that does not effect a change of
v̇ạ̣̇l̇ẹ̇n̈ce preserves logical equivalence. For example the equation
$-[-\quad) - (+y)] = +[+(+y) - (+x)]$ has convalent sides, and it is
algeḃ. ̣lly correct. This guarantees the equivalence of the two
propos̤ị̣ạ̣ons that are represented: 'not every un-x isn't y'
and 'some y isn't x'. We therefore extend the Principle of Equivalence to include all categoricals, primitive or derived:

*PE   Categorical propositions are logically equivalent if and only
if they are equal and convalent.*

The Principle of Equivalence may be applied to any inference
called "immediate" in traditional logic. An immediate inference
has a single premise and a single conclusion. When an immediate
inference is valid, the converse inference from the conclusion to
the premise is also valid. The propositions of a valid immediate
inference are thus logically equivalent and subject to the Principle of Equivalence.

We have now extended the logical syntax to propositions containing 'some' and 'every'. The general form of proposition is

$$\pm [\pm(\pm x) \pm (\pm y)]$$

yes/no [some/every(x/un-x) is/isn't (y/un-y)].

The forms of natural language suppress the positive signs. Only
'some', which is positive, is made explicit to contrast it with
'every'. In the case where no contrast is relevant, neither sign of
quantity occurs. As we shall see, this is the case with singular
subjects (including singular phrases like 'the waiter') and it is
the case in certain "indefinite" propositions where one or the
other sign is understood (babies were crying, whales are mam-
mals). In general, except for 'some', positive signs are usually
suppressed; there are no positive prefixes and there is no standard sign of affirmation corresponding to the sign for propositional denial.

In arithmetic practice, an expression like $+[-(+x) + (+y)]$
would be reduced to $-x + y$. This is already true for 'every A is

B'. If we use direct transcription we render this as $-x + y$. As mentioned above, the sentence 'some A is B' has a "redundant" positive sign; this is the exception to the rule removing all algebraically redundant signs. Using the natural economies of notation and direct transcription, we can formulate several equivalent schedules of four categoricals. (A less traditionally prejudiced scheduling would include propositions with negative terms in subject and predicate positions as well.)

every x is y	$-x + y$	every x is y	$-x + y$
every x isn't y	$-x - y$	not some x is y	$-(+x + y)$
some x is y	$+x + y$	some x is y	$+x + y$
some x isn't y	$+x - y$	not every x is y	$-(-x + y)$

not some x is un-y	$-(+x + (-y))$
every x is un-y	$-x + (-y)$
not every x is un-y	$-(-x + (-y))$
some x is un-y	$+x + (-y)$

The standard traditional schedule is

every x is y	$-x + y$
no x is y	$-(x + y)$
some x is y	$+x + y$
some x isn't y	$+x - y$

Algebraic analysis of the traditional schedule reveals its formal inelegance as compared with any of the three preceding schedules. The first schedule is illuminating because it clearly exhibits contrariety: two propositions with the same subject phrase that have predicate phrases of opposite quality are contrary. The second schedule illuminates contradiction; the last in connection with the first two schedules exhibits the law of predicate obversion, the equivalence of 'isn't x' and 'is un-x'.

More explicit formulations that do not take advantage of the usual notational economies have certain theoretical advantages. In the immediately ensuing paragraphs we shall often revert to the less economical and more explicit formulations.

Current theories of logical form distinguish singular propositions from general propositions, and atomic propositions from molecular propositions. In algebraic transcription, these different kinds of propositions have the same general form: $\pm [\pm(\pm x) \pm (\pm y)]$.

Singular Propositions. In traditional logic, singular and general propositions do not differ in logical form. The laws of syllogistic and immediate inference require the convertibility of terms and this means that singular terms may also appear in predicate position. Nothing in natural syntax prohibits this. Singular terms differ from general terms in not being preceded by the signs of quantity ('some' and 'every'). But the reason for this is thought to be semantic and not syntactic. It is just because 'every x_i is y' is always equivalent to 'some x_i is y' (where 'x_i' is a singular term) that the words of quantity for singular propositions are omitted in natural language. If so, the logical form of 'Socrates is mortal' is '$\pm S_i + M$'. The sign of double quantity is used to indicate that the singular proposition is *indifferently* universal or particular. The subscript 'i' marks the singular term and it licenses the use of either sign of quantity for purposes of inference. The view that singular propositions are doubly general may be found in Leibniz:

> Some logical difficulties worth solution have occurred to me. How is it that opposition is valid in the case of singular propositions—e.g., 'Peter is a soldier' and 'Peter is not a soldier'—since everywhere else a universal affirmative and a particular negative are opposed? Should we say that a singular proposition is equivalent to a particular and to a universal proposition? Yes, we should. So when it is objected that a singular proposition is equivalent to a particular proposition, since the conclusion in the third figure must be particular and can nevertheless be singular, e.g., 'every writer is a man, some writer is Peter, therefore Peter is a man'. I reply that here also the conclusion is also particular; and it is as if we had drawn the conclusion 'some Peter is a man'. For 'some Peter' and 'every Peter' coincide since the term is singular.[3]

The doctrine that singular propositions have "wild" quantity has logical consequences that Leibniz did not foresee. We are here concerned with the fact that singular propositions are comprehended under the general form of proposition $\pm[\pm(\pm x) \pm (\pm y)]$. In explicit form 'Socrates is mortal' can be given two representations; $+[+(+S_i) + (+M)]$ and $+[-(+S_i) + (+M)]$. In practice we shall use an abbreviated form with the double sign of quantity: $\pm S_i + M$. Because singular terms can appear in predicate position, the singular proposition 'Tully is Cicero'

3. Ibid., p. 115.

comes under the general form. Its explicit transcription is
$+[+(+T_i) + (+C_i)]$. The abbreviated form is $\pm T_i + C_i$.

Existence Propositions.   Identity propositions thus receive a
subject-predicate formulation that directly transcribes the vernacular. The same is true for propositions that predicate the
verb 'exists'. In traditional logic, the sentence 'some black swans
exist' is regimented as 'some black swans are existent'. In our
notation the transcription is '$+BS + E$'. Similarly, 'Pegasus does
not exist' is transcribed as '$-(\pm P_i + E)$'. As we use the label, an
existence proposition is a proposition that predicates 'exists'
overtly. The standard particular proposition 'some swans are
black' is not in this sense an existence proposition. However,
existence propositions are comprehended in the general form of
proposition.

Propositions with Compound Terms.   A compound term is a
term of form 'x and y' or 'x or y'. In logical algebra, the word
'and' is transcribed by a plus sign. Since 'and' is often used as a
synonym for 'plus' in the sense of addition, this assignment is
entirely natural. We shall also see that it preserves logical relationships in algebraic form. The conjunctive form 'x and y' is
transcribed thus: $\langle +x + y \rangle$. We use angular brackets to distinguish compound terms from propositions.

We have added an initial plus sign to indicate the analogy between the forms for 'some . . . is . . .' and 'and'. The analogy is
important; just as particular forms are positive in valence, so are
conjunctions. Disjunctions on the other hand are negative. To
get an algebraic representation for disjunction, we use a method
similar to the one used when we defined 'every . . . is . . . ', using
a primitive predication containing the signs 'not' and 'is'. In the
present case the defining expression contains the signs 'not'
and 'and'. The expression is 'not (both) not-x and not-y':
$-\langle +(-x) + (-y) \rangle$. Now this formula represents a compound that is
logically equivalent to 'x or y'. And the formula itself is algebraically equal to $\langle -(-x) + y \rangle$. We therefore take this new formula
to represent 'x or y'. For purposes of exhibiting the symmetry of
'or' we shall also use the form '$\langle -(-x) - (-y) \rangle$'.

It is clear that compound terms themselves have the same form
as propositions. This fact is of significance for the theory of
deep structure which often traces the analysis of a compound
expression to a sentence source in the base. For example, the
phrase 'wise man' is traced to 'a man is wise'. Since 'man and
wise' and 'a man is wise' have the same form $(+M + W)$ the
assignment of this sort of base is structurally sound.

The general form of a compound expression is $\pm\langle\pm(\pm x) \pm (\pm y)\rangle$. In reckoning with compounds we must observe the same valence constraint as with propositions. Conjunctions are positive, disjunctions are negative. Neither may be equated with the other. On the other hand, any algebraic operation that preserves valence is logically effective. For example, the propositions 'every x is y and not-x' and 'everything that is z or not-y is not-x' are logically equivalent. The equivalence is algebraic:

$$-x + \langle +y + (-z)\rangle = -\langle-(+y + (-z))\rangle + (-x) = -\langle-(-z) + (-y)\rangle + (-x).$$

Compound Propositions.   Compound propositions are no exception to the rule that all propositions have the form $\pm (\pm(\pm x) \pm (\pm y))$. In the case of compound propositions the letters 'x' and 'y' stand for propositions and not terms. And the meaning of the signs is different. Thus the function '$-p + q$' is not read as 'every p is q' but as 'if p then q'. Nevertheless the form is the same. We shall use square brackets for propositional expressions. Even complicated compounds are comprehended under the general form. For example, the function 'if p and q then r or s' is represented as $-[+p + q] + [-(-r) + s]$.

The general form of compound propositions is $\pm[\pm(\pm p) \pm (\pm q)]$. In reckoning with compound expressions we apply a notational rule which permits the iteration of an element to form a conjunction or disjunction. The rule permits the substitution of 'x and x' or 'x or x' for 'x'. The laws that are basic to arithmetic or algebra are fundamental here too. The fundamental laws are association and commutation (for disjunction and conjunction) and distribution. Algebraic operations are subject to the valence constraint which prohibits equivalences between conjunctions and disjunctions except where explicitly licensed by distribution.

A proposition that has the form '$-x + x$' is a tautology. A more general tautological form is $-y + [-x + x]$. By applying the familiar algebraic operations (association, etc.), it is always possible to reduce a tautological function to an expression that has the canonical form of a tautology.

Relational Propositions.   Examples of propositions that contain relational terms are

(1) Some sailor reads a (certain) poem to every girl.

(2) Everyone who draws a circle draws a figure.

(3) Some boy is taller than every girl.

These are transcribed in a straightforward fashion.

1. $+ S + r + P - G$

2. $- (d + C) + (d + F)$

3. $+ B + t - G$

If we negate (1) we get $-(S + r + P - G)$, which says that no sailor reads a poem to every girl. This proposition is logically equivalent to 'every sailor fails-to-read every poem to some girl'. Once again we find the algebra logically perspicuous in expressing the equivalence:

$$-(S + r + P - G) = -S + (-r) - P + G.$$

As (2) illustrates, a relational term can occur in either subject or predicate position. Relational propositions are no exception to the rule that all propositions have the general form $\pm[\pm(\pm x) \pm (\pm y)]$. Moreover, the algebraic transcription of relational propositions is logically effective and clear. The clarity is exhibited in the resolution of a structurally ambiguous sentence such as 'Sam did not hit a target.' It has two possible transcriptions:

(i) $S_i - h + T$

(ii) $S_i - (h + T)$.

It is commonly assumed that a logical syntax along traditional (Leibnizian) lines must fail to disambiguate a sentence like 'every boy loves some girl', which may on the one hand be interpreted to say of some girl that she is loved by every boy and, on the other hand, to say of every boy that he loves a girl (some girl or other). In the first case we give 'some girl' a specific reading (some girl = a certain girl). In the second case we give 'some girl' a nonspecific reading (some girl = some girl or other). In the notation we have devised, the difference between the specific and nonspecific reading would be decided by the order in which the subjects 'every boy' and 'some girl' appear in the transcription. The transcription of 'every boy loves some girl or other' is '$-B + l_1 + G$'. The transcription of 'some girl is loved by every boy' is '$+G + l_2 - B$'.

In algebraic transcription every subject is either positive or negative, having the form 'x' or '$-x$'. A relational sentence has two or more subjects, and a positive subject may be specific or nonspecific. The rule for a nonspecific reading is this:

A positive subject is nonspecific if and only if it is preceded by but not followed by a negative subject.

This rule corresponds to the convention, in standard logical grammars, for reading the existential quantifiers that is preceded by but not followed by a universal quantifier. Thus '$(x) \exists y (Lxy)$' is the translation of 'everyone loves someone or other' just as '$-P + l_1 + P$' is the transcription of 'every person loves some person or other'. '$\exists x(y)(Lyx)$' is the translation of 'someone is loved by everyone'. Its algebraic transcription is '$+P + l_2 - P$'. Note that the transcription makes use of the converse form 'is loved by' (l_2). In the standard logical language the explicit use of the converse (passive) form is avoided. The effect of the converse is achieved by the difference in the order of 'x' and 'y' as these appear in the quantifiers and in the matrix. Thus 'Lyx' can be read as 'x is loved by y', and when the order of letters in the quantifiers is 'x, y' we so read it.

In algebraic transcription, as in the vernacular, the converse form is explicitly used and we rely on the analytic relations between the forms 'loves' and 'is loved by'. In general, if R_1 is an n-place relation, it will belong to a set $R_1 \ldots R_{n!}$ any two of whose members are converse to each other. For example, there are $3!$ ways of ordering the subjects of '$\ldots$ gives $\ldots$ to $\ldots$' and so there are six sentences beginning with 'some x gives some y to some z' ($+x + G_1 + y + z$) and ending with 'some z gets some y from some x' ($+z + G_6 + y + x$), any two of which are analytically equivalent to one another. Schemas of this kind are analytically equivalent whenever the quantity of the subjects is uniform. Thus 'every boy loves every girl' and 'every girl is loved by every boy' are analytically equivalent, but 'every boy loves some girl' and 'some girl is loved by every boy' are not equivalent.

As another illustration of the ability of the algebraic notation to disambiguate the specific and nonspecific senses of 'some x', consider the difference between a sailor who reads a certain poem to each and every girl and one who reads every girl some poem or other. We use (1) to describe the former and (1*) to describe the latter.

1. $+S + r_1 + P - G$

1*. $+ S + r_2 - G + P$

Sentences containing pronouns.   In translations from the vernacular a pronoun that is not cross-referential to a proper name will appear as a bound variable. The translation is said to reveal the logical form of the translated sentence, and it is widely assumed that the grammars of natural languages obscure the true nature of pronouns precisely because they lack a standardized apparatus corresponding to the apparatus of quantifiers and variables of the standard logical languagees that serves to make the nature of pronominalization explicit. We have then the thesis that pronouns (at bottom and unsuperficially) *are* bound variables and that this is explicated in logical translation.

If this thesis were correct the prospect would be dim indeed for a logical syntax of natural language, for we could not represent pronouns in our logical grammar without some device comparable to the quantifier variable notation, and this mode of representation is a radical departure from the grammars of natural language. Once again we seem to be faced with the choice between, on the one hand, accepting an unnatural but highly perspicuous and logically effective way of representing the logical form of a significant kind of discourse, and, on the other, some more natural traditional way which is logically vague and semantically unperspicuous. Fortunately for the Leibnizian program, it is not hard to find a logically effective way of representing pronouns that is close to the natural grammars. As for the bound variable view, it suffers from more than artificiality. I shall briefly discuss one grave objection to it. There are others.

If pronouns are bound variables, they must occur in the same sentence as the antecedent subject which binds them and which they pronominalize. For example, 'Some man is at the door. He is armed.' becomes 'some man$_x$ (x is at the door and x is armed)', where the pronoun 'he' refers back to 'some man' and is seen to be bound by it. It is clear that any such binding requires that the pronoun and its antecedent be in the same sentence. Unfortunately for the bound variable theory of pronouns, it is, as often as not, simply not possible to construe pronominalization as taking place within a single sentence. Thus consider

Some man is at the door. Is he armed?
Some man is at the door. Arm him!
Some man is at the door. So he climbed all those stairs.

In such cases it is not open to us to form a syntactical union of the sentence containing the pronoun with the sentence containing the antecedent. Nor is it plausible to say that 'he' in 'so he climbed all those stairs' differs in logical form from 'he' in

'and he climbed all those stairs'. Similarly 'he' in 'is he armed?'
cannot differ from 'he' in 'he is armed'. Since 'he' in 'is he
armed?' is not a bound variable, it is not a bound variable in 'he
is armed', and we ought to look for another way of understanding the pronouns of the natural languages. This is not to say that
we cannot, for certain logical purposes, translate 'he' as a bound
variable. But we should do so with the awareness that our
"translation," however useful, cannot be faithful to the original.
The fact that the translation cannot be carried through in in-
numerable cases in which the pronoun has exactly the same
meaning as it has in some case for which the translation can be
made to work should give pause to anyone who holds to the
idea that translation as a bound variable reveals the nature of
the pronoun in the vernacular.

According to the traditional doctrine, every logical subject is
of form 'every x' or 'some x'. We apply this doctrine to pronouns
and distinguish between the logical sign of the pronoun and the
term (or proterm) that follows the sign. Thus the word 'he' in
(4) can be taken as a whole subject to its logical form will include a sign of quantity, or it can be taken as the term that
follows the (implicit) sign of quantity. The ambiguity of 'he' is
similar to the ambiguity of 'Socrates' in subject position. For
'Socrates' can be taken as a whole subject with implicit quantity,
or it can be taken simply as a singular term. Because every logical
subject consists of a sign of quantity followed by a term, the
traditional theory distinguishes between the modes of signification of the whole subject and the term it contains. Let *reference*
be the mode of signification of a subject and *denotation* be the
mode of signification of a term. In 'some man is at the door' the
subject 'some man' *refers* to some man in a nonidentifying way;
the term 'man' *denotes* all men. A term is said to be distributed
in a subject when the reference of the subject coincides with the
denotation of the term; otherwise the term is said to be undis-
tributed. Consider again the pronoun 'he' in (4). Taken as a
whole subject, 'he' refers to whatever the antecedent refers to,
that is, it refers to "the man in question." Taken as the term of
this subject (the proterm), 'he' also *denotes* what is referred to
by the antecedent subject. This is generally true of the proterm:
it is defined to denote what the antecedent subject *refers* to. Thus
every proterm is distributed in its pronoun and every pronoun
has universal quantity in addition to the quantity of the antecedent subject. In effect, the pronoun for a definite subject
'some x' will always be an expression with "wild" quantity.
Pronouns that cross-refer to 'every x' are another matter. They

of course will have universal quantity. But the assignment of particular quantity to a pronoun whose antecedent is universal is unjustified in those cases where this would confer existential import on the sentence containing the pronomial subject. In such cases the assignment of particular quantity would illegitimately give the pronoun a mode of signification that is stronger than that possessed by its antecedent subject.

In the algebraic transcriptions of pronouns, we must have some way of indicating the cross-reference of the pronoun to the antecedent. To this end we affix to the antecedent subject a letter as an index. The occurrence of the letter attached to a subject will anticipate its subsequent pronominalization. We then use the same letter, only capitalized, for the proterm of the pronoun. For example, "Ed came. Is he drunk?" would be transcribed thus:

$$\pm E_i + c. \quad ? \pm I + D?$$

Other examples of transcribed pronominalization are

Tom loves himself

$$\pm T_i + l_1 \pm I$$

every owner of a donkey beats it

$$-(O + D_j) + b \pm J$$

if some being is divine then no other being is

$$-[+B_k + D] + [-((-K) + D)]$$

a boy who was fooling her kissed a girl who trusted him

$$+\langle +B_c + (f \pm M)\rangle + k + \langle + G_m + (t \pm C)\rangle$$

The idea of logical syntax in natural language is supported by evidence that algebraic transcription expresses familiar logical relationships. The difference between the standard logical translations and the logical transcriptions can hardly be exaggerated. Take for example the sentence form 'every A is B'. Its albegraic form is '$-A + B$'. Its canonical form is '$(x)\, (A_x \supset B_x)$'. The first is a *transcription* of the vernacular; it is read *as we read* the vernacular. Since it is algebraic, it expresses a formal aspect of the syntax of the vernacular. Moreover, the syntax is logical syntax in the literal sense; it is effective in logical reckoning. The quantificational formula is also logically effective but it is a *translation* or paraphrase of the vernacular original. The translation makes use of new syntactical elements not found in the original. It may be tempting to think of the canonical formula as a transcription, a formal reading of the original sentence. Thus Strawson calls the function '$A_x \supset B_x$' the predicative formula. But if one thinks of '(x)' as transcribing 'every' and of '$A_x \supset B_x$' as transcribing 'A is B' then what is one to make of 'A is B' as it occurs in 'some A is B'?

The difference between translation and transcription is even more clear in the case of relational sentences. Compare the transcription of '$+S + r + P - G$' with its canonical rendering

$$(\exists x)\,(\exists y)\,[Sx \cdot Py \cdot \ (z)\,(Gz \supset Rxyz)].$$

The quantificational formula is a translation into a language that is logically powerful and syntactically novel. Nevertheless, to say that this formula represents *the* logical form of the original sentence 'some sailor read a (certain) poem to every girl' is unwarranted. What is wrong with the logical form of the sentence itself as made explicit by '$+S + r + P - G$? We shall presently see that the transcriptional form is just as powerful for purposes of logical reckoning and it retains the syntax of the sentence intact.

The disparity between natural language and the formulas of modern logic is dramatic when the ingenious devices for ordering quantifiers come into play. But the monadic cases already represent a crucial departure. Once quantifiers are used all the sentences of logic are formulated in a way that overtly affirms or denies the existence of certain things. Canonical form thus introduces a pervasive ontological idiom into logic. In natural language existence claims are exceptional. We could say that some ideal gases are colorless without meaning to say that such gases exist. In the algebraic representation the difference would be reflected in the two forms

1. $+IG + (-C)$

2. $+\langle+IG + (-C)\rangle + E.$

In the second formula, the predicate '$+E$' stands for 'exists' or 'is existent'.

The gap between a natural logical syntax and the current canonical syntax of predicate logic is also evident in the fact that some sentences of natural language are not translatable into the technical idiom of the latter language. We do say things like 'Pegasus does not exist'. By the formation rules of a standard logic without identity this cannot be translated. Two prohibitions prevent it. First, since 'Pegasus' is an individual symbol it cannot occupy a predicate position. And second, 'exists' is not a predicate.

The same formation rules that preclude the predication of singular terms preclude the appearance of a general term in subject position. It is therefore impossible to construe 'men are mortal' on a par with 'Socrates is mortal'. The alleged difference of logical form is not something discovered; it is written into modern logic at the level of the formation rules. Geach and Strawson, among many other philosophers, have offered semantic arguments for the syntactical gap between two sorts of expressions, one of which is predicable and incomplete, while the other is nominal and complete. But all their arguments initially take for granted that it is absurd to predicate 'is x' of a subject when 'x' is an individual symbol. In effect they beg the question by assuming the absurdity of allowing singular terms the same syntactical positions as general terms. One consequence of this assumption is the reading given to 'Tully is Cicero' and other sentences that seem to have singular terms in both subject and predicate positions. Such sentences can no longer be taken at face value; the doctrine of the 'is' of identity is invoked to save the dogma that singular terms cannot occupy predicate position.

Semantic theories to the side, the syntactic issue is clear enough. No one has ever seen an 'is' of identity no matter how long he stared. The idea that the 'is' of 'a is b' *must* mean '=' has its origin in the deeply rooted dogmatic syntactical doctrine: if both 'a' and 'b' are individual symbols (singular terms), the sentence is literally ill formed. Thus if a sentence of this form is assumed to be well formed, the 'is' must somehow be construed as a relational expression of form 'is R to'. Since sentences like 'Tully is Cicero' do make sense, we must somehow read them as dyadic. Hence the " 'is' of identity." So understood, the relation of identity is a new primitive of logic and a number of axioms governing it are needed. In contrast to this standard theory, the notion of identity in a traditional logic is not primitive; identity may be *defined* as holding between a and b *whenever it is monadically true that a is b*. We shall see below that the theory of identity as defined in terms of monadic predication is also less prodigal in needing no special axioms. Indeed all the desired laws of identity can be derived from the traditional bases of immediate and syllogistic inference.

We now present additional evidence of the logical usefulness of algebraic transcription for reckoning familiar kinds of arguments. Perhaps the most surprising feature of the plus-minus notation is its extension to logical signs that are not ordinarily thought of as either positive or negative. We do think of 'is' as a positive copula and of 'isn't' as a negative copula. But we don't think of 'some' as a positive word of quantity or of 'every' as a negative word of quantity. Intuition does not prepare us for this quickchange of quantity into quality. In particular, the discovery that 'every' is a minus sign is far from being an "aha" experience. It is only when we continue to investigate the role of 'every' in inference that this novel idea becomes clearer and more acceptable.

Textbooks of traditional logic begin with immediate inference and go on to syllogistic. The theory of immediate inference is encompassed in the Principle of Equivalence: one categorical follows from another when and only when the two categoricals are equal and convalent. The theory of syllogistic reasoning is encompassed when we add the *Dictum de Omni*. This Dictum—in its algebraic form—will give us further insight into the negative character of 'every'.

According to Aristotle and his medieval followers, the *Dictum de Omni* is the basic principle of syllogistic reasoning. The *Dictum* has had a bad press, mainly because of poor formulation. The following formulation captures the Dictum with adequate Precision:

D. *What is true of* every x *is true of what* is x.

The *Dictum* asserts a cancellation relation between 'every x' and 'is x'. It could be called "the every–is cancellation principle" or—with additional allusion to its eminent place in traditional logical theory—"the Everest Principle." Applying D to 'is mortal' (true of *every* human) and to Socrates (who *is* human) we conclude that 'is mortal' is true of Socrates. The 'every/is' cancellation is evident if we write the syllogism as a sum in which the middle phrases disappear:

	every human is mortal
Socrates	is human
Socrates	is mortal.

More generally the Everest Principle asserts the validity of all syllogisms in the omnibus form:

$-x \pm z$		every x is/isn't z
$\pm y + x$	some/every y	is x
$\pm y \quad \pm z$	some/every y	is/isn't z.

A syllogism of a form like this will be called canonically valid. In a canonical syllogism 'every x' cancels 'is x', and the predicate of the major is added to the subject of the minor premise to form the conclusion.

It is clear from the canonical forms that the role of 'every' in syllogistic inference is that of a negative sign opposed to the positive copula 'is'. If 'is' is given a plus rendering, 'every' must be given a minus rendering. The plus-minus opposition of 'is' and 'every' is also exhibited in the basic tautological form 'every x is x'. Some philosophers are fond of saying that tautologies "say nothing." In the algebraic form '$-x + x$', this looks literally true.

The Everest Principle implicitly stipulates three conditions for syllogistic validity:

1. A valid syllogism has at least one universal premise (an "omni" premise).
2. The conclusion is convalent with the other premise (the "est" premise).
3. The sum of the premises is equal to the conclusion.

These three conditions are necessary *and sufficient* for validity. Obviously not all valid syllogisms are in canonically valid form. But *any* syllogism that is valid, any syllogism that satisfies the three conditions, can be expressed in canonical form through the use of the Equivalence Principle. For example, a syllogism of form

> every z is non-x
> not every y is non-x
> _____
> some y isn't z

is transcribed thus:

$$-z + (-x) \qquad\qquad -x - z$$
$$\underline{-(-y + (-x))} \qquad\qquad \underline{+y + x}$$
$$+y - z \qquad\qquad +y - z \quad.$$

The right side shows the equivalence of the propositions of this syllogism to the propositions of a canonically valid syllogism.

By a syllogism we shall now mean any syllogistic argument of n propositions and n terms including those arguments called Sorites (where $n > 3$). By the two valence conditions only two kinds of syllogistic arguments are candidates for validity:

1. syllogisms that contain no particular propositions.
2. syllogisms with a particular conclusion and exactly one particular premise.

Let us call any syllogism "regular" if it is one of these two kinds.

The condition for syllogistic validity may now be stated for any syllogistic argument of n propositions. A syllogistic argument '$P_1 \ldots P_{n-1}$, therefore C' is valid if and only if

1. the argument is regular
2. $P_1 + \ldots + P_{n-1} = C$.

The test for validity is very easy to apply. First one inspects the syllogism for regularity. If the syllogism is regular, one simply takes the sum of the premises to see whether they add up to the conclusion. If and only if the syllogism passes both these tests is it valid.

Enthymemes.   Henceforth we shall write syllogisms as equations. The plus sign between two premises represents 'and'. The equal sign may be read as 'hence', and it should not be assumed that it is symmetrical. Using equations we can solve for the missing premises of arguments that are assumed valid but that do not have the same number of premises as they have terms. Here is an example: "some clergymen are popes and every pope is a bachelor; hence some clergymen are not married." This argument is valid but it has a missing premise. Let the missing premise be '$\pm x \pm y$'. The argument now is

$$+[\pm x \pm y] + [+C + P] + [-P + B] = [+C - M].$$

Solving for the missing premise we find

$$\pm x + y = +C - M - C - P + P - B = -M - B = -B - M = -B + (-M).$$

The missing premise is 'every bachelor is unmarried'.

We now consider a number of enthymemes that are of considerable logical importance.

1. The argument form 'every A is B, hence some A is B' is valid only if it is assumed to be an enthymeme with a missing premise, 'some A is A'. The truth conditions of 'some A is A' may vary. This schema therefore ought not to be treated as logically valid.

2. The argument 'everything is created, hence the sun is created' is a valid enthymeme. Let the missing premise be $\pm x \pm y$. The equation is

$$[\pm x \pm y] + [-T + C] = [\pm S_i + C]$$

$$\pm x \pm y = +S_i + C + T - C = \pm S_i + T.$$

The missing premise is 'the sun is a thing', a platitude that we may take as true.

3. The argument 'the sun is created, hence something is created' is also valid if we add the premise 'the sun is a thing':

$$[-S_i + C] + [+S_i + T] = [+T + C].$$

4. The argument 'the sun is created, hence some created thing exists' needs the premise 'the sun exists' for validity. The argument is not logically valid:

$$[+S_i + E] + [-S_i + C] = [+C + E].$$

Notice that both (3) and (4) make use of the valence license accorded to singular propositions. The subject phrase 'the sun' is given a universal sign in one premise and a particular sign in the other premise. This enables us to cancel it out.

5. The cogito "I think, I am" is sometimes viewed as an enthymeme: 'I think, Hence I am'. The missing premise would then be 'every thinker is existent':

$$[\pm I_i + T] + [-T + E] = [\pm I_i + E].$$

The Principles of Identity.   The identity relation is defined thus:

$$a = b   =\text{df. a is b}$$

Since 'a is b' is a singular proposition, it has "wild" quantity. We may therefore represent it either as '$+a + b$' or as '$-a + b$', depending on which expression we need for purposes of inference. The identity definition may also be stated thus:

$$a = b   =\text{df. } \pm a + b$$

The principles of identity are theorems derivable from the rules of immediate and syllogistic inference. The exception is the law of reflexivity, which is immediately seen to be a tautology of form 'every x is x'.

1. *Identity is reflexive:*

$$a = a = \text{df} - a + a$$

$$- a + a \quad \text{Tautology}$$

2. *Identity is symmetrical:*

$$a = b   \therefore   b = a$$

$$a = b   = \text{df. } + a + b$$

$$b = a   = \text{df. } + b + a$$

$$+a + b   = +b + a \qquad \text{(by Equivalence)   Q.E.D.}$$

3. *Identity is transitive:*

(a = b) and (b = c), hence a = c.

Using the definition 'x = y = df. −x + y' we get a valid syllogism:

$$−a + b$$
$$\underline{−b + c}$$
$$−a + c \qquad \text{Q.E.D.}$$

4. *Indiscernibles are identical:*
The assumption that '*a*' and '*b*' are indiscernible amounts to this: if '*a*' and '*b*' are singular terms and '*P*' is any term, then −[±*a* + *P*] + [±*b* + *P*]. In particular, if we substitute '*a*' in the predicate position we get −[−*a* + *a*] + [−*b* + *a*]. Since the antecedent is tautological by (1), the consequent is true. But the consequent asserts the identity of *b* and *a*.

5. *Identicals are indiscernible:*
This asserts that if '*a*' and '*b*' are singular and '*P*' is any term, then the syllogism '*a* is identical with *b* and *a* is *P*, hence *b* is *P*' is valid. Using the definition of identity and setting '*a* = *b*' equivalent to 'every *a* is *b*' we have the valid syllogism:

$$−a + b$$
$$\underline{+a + P}$$
$$+b + P.$$

It is evident that a formalization of traditional logic along Leibnizian lines does not require certain extra assumptions common to modern logical systems. Using the Principle of Equivalence as the rule for immediate inference, and the Dictum cancellation rule for syllogistic inference, we find no need for special principles of existential generalization or universal instantiation, nor do we need special axioms for the identity relation. The traditional approach is especially noteworthy for its ability to block the inference from 'Pegasus is a flying horse' (which we may consider true) to 'a flying horse exists'. The traditional way of getting existence propositions from singular propositions is enthymemic. For the inference to go through we would need the premise 'Pegasus exists'. Since this premise is false, the inference is unsound. In standard systems of current logic, the proposition 'Pegasus is a flying horse' is (gratuitously) viewed as false on pain of allowing the unwanted conclusion 'a flying horse exists'.

We now illustrate the reckoning of a number of arguments of

various kinds. Some of these arguments use principles that go beyond the rules we have so far given. But only a hint of their justification can be offered here.[4]

1.   every A is B and C $-A + \langle +B + C\rangle$
      every B is D $-B + D$
      ─────────────   ─────────────
      every A is D and C $-A + \langle +D + C\rangle$

2.   every A is B
      every C is D
      ─────────────

      every A and C is B and D.

To validate (2) we add the analytic premise 'every A and C is A and C'. We then apply the principle illustrated in (1):

$$-\langle +A + C\rangle + \langle +A + C\rangle$$
$$-A + B$$
$$-C + D$$
$$\overline{}$$
$$-\langle +A + C\rangle + \langle +B + D\rangle$$

3. Every circle is a figure, hence everyone who draws a circle draws a figure.

$$- C + F$$
$$-(D + C) + (D + C)$$
$$\overline{}$$
$$-(D + C) + (D + F)$$

4.   some cheetah is faster than every horse
      some horse is faster than some man
      ───────────────────────────────────

      some cheetah is faster than some man

For this argument we add a premise that is analytic for transitive relations:

> if every horse is faster than some man then everything faster than some horse is faster than some man.

The general definition of transitive R is

$-[\pm A + R \pm B] + [-(R \pm A) + (R \pm B)]$ if some/every A is R to some/every B then whatever is R to every/some A is R to some/every B.

─────────────────────

4. For further discussion on the validation of arguments in algebraic form, see the authors "Calculus of Terms," "The Logical and the Extra-Logical," and "Distribution Matters."

Applying the definition of a transitive relation to the second premise gives us the premise we need:

$$+C + f - H$$
$$+H + f + M$$
$$\underline{-[-H + f + M] + [-(f - H) + (f + M)]}$$
$$+C + f + M.$$

The next example answers the oft-repeated charge that a traditional logic must prove incapable of handling inferences like 'some girl is loved by every boy; so every boy loves some girl or other'. The proof exploits the wild quantity of pronominalizations of 'some girl'. The second, third, and fourth premises are truisms. The second premise reads 'she is a girl'. The consequent of the fourth premise reads 'every boy loves her'.

$$1. \ +G_i + l_2 - B$$
$$2. \ +I + G$$
$$3. \ -[+G_i + l_2 - B] + [-I + l_2 - B]$$
$$\underline{4. \ -[-I + l_2 - B] + [-B + l_1 - I]}$$
$$- B + l_1 + G$$

When an indexed nominal expression is replaced by cancelation, the pronoun that refers to it will now refer to the new nominal that replaces it. For example, from the premises 'every man loves himself; Cicero is a man' we can infer 'Cicero loves *him*self', and the pronoun in the conclusion now has cross-reference to 'Cicero' which has replaced 'every man' by cancelation:

$$-M_j + l \pm J$$
$$\underline{\pm C + M}$$
$$\pm C_j + l \pm J$$

In traditional logic an identity proposition is a monadic proposition with singular terms in both subject and predicate positions. The final example exploits this and shows how to get by without treating identity as a relation governed by special axioms. In the proof we have added a truistic third premise which reads: if Cicero is envious of everyone else (everyone not himself) then Cicero is envious of everyone other than Cicero (everyone who is not Cicero):

1. every senator is envious of everyone else
2. Cicero is a senator
3. Cicero is not envious of Tully

   Tully is Cicero

1. $-S_i + e - (-I)$

2. $\pm C + S$

3. $-[\pm C_i + e - (-I)] + [\pm C_i + e - (-C_i)]$

4. $\pm C_i + (-e) \pm T$

   $\pm T + C_i$

Summary Discussion.   I began by comparing the programs of Frege and Leibniz in the area of logical syntax. This led to the development of a notational suggestion of Leibniz whose aim was to show that a good notation could help to reinstate the Leibnizian ideal of a logical syntax of natural language. The transcriptional character of this notation and its logical effectiveness significantly contribute to the justification of the traditional idea that the natural languages have a logical syntax close to the surface syntax. In this connection it was noted earlier that the more artificial standard languages achieved acceptance because of the inference power of the logics which made use of their grammars. I believe this to be the main cause of the initial triumph of Russell's crusade on behalf of Frege's logical syntax. Today one would point as well to other virtues of the standard logical grammar. Thus Quine remarks:

> The grammar that we logicians tendentiously call standard is a grammar designed with no other thought than to facilitate the tracing of truth conditions. And a very good thought this is.[5]

As an example of the advantage of standard grammar over the grammar of natural language, consider the sentence 'an American has walked on the moon'. The sentence has no part that explicitly signifies the existence of Americans. The existence of an American is, however, a condition for the truth of the statement made with the sentence, and its canonical translation says as much. Frege's conceptual script has the virtue of semantic explicitness, a desideratum that is deemed essential to the claim

5. W. V. Quine, *The Philosophy of Logic* (Englewood Cliffs, N.J.: Prentice-Hall, Inc., 1970), p. 35.

that it is a logical syntax. As Quine puts it: "logic chases truth up
the tree of grammar." Once again we seem to be faced with an
attractive and well entrenched idea that would spell doom for
the idea of a logical syntax of natural language. For it is a fact
that the natural languages are not semantically explicit at the
level of syntax. The matter at issue here is deserving of extended
discussion. For reasons of space my rejoinder must be peremp-
torily brief.

A sentence of form 'some x is y' or 'the x is y' is said to have
existential import if the statement made by its use cannot be
true unless some x (the x) exists. It is undoubtedly true that
many such sentences have existential import. But if we parse all
such sentences to make this condition explicit and then treat
the parsing as a presentation of logical form, we find ourselves
forced to judge certain statements false that do not have the existence of (an) x as a condition of truth. We are, for example,
constrained to judge 'some frictionless motion on an inclined
surface is constant' to be false on the grounds that there is no
such motion anywhere in nature even though this sentence can
be used to assert a truth in physics. We are similarly constrained
to consider 'the beast captured by Bellerophon is a flying horse'
false although we demand the opposite judgment of a student
taking a "true-false" examination in classics. It is a familiar fact
that sentences in the vernacular of form 'some x is y' often lack
existential import. Even so, no one would deny that all such
sentences have the same logical form. The same is true of sentences of form 'the x is y' or 'a is y' (where 'a' is a proper name).
For we should like to give the same syntactical analysis to 'the
beast captured by Bellerophon is a flying horse' as to 'the
thirty-seventh president of the United States is a Republican'
while allowing for the truth of both. Sentences of form 'the/
some x is y' have a variety of truth conditions, and the use of
truth conditions to determine logical syntax is a questionable
practice even when accompanied by the disclaimer that the expression whose syntax is semantically explicit is not meant to
be faithful to the natural syntax of the original. We have already observed that this practice introduces a pervasive and con-
stricting ontological idiom into logical suntax. In natural languages there is a clear distinction between 'the/some x is y' and
'the/some x that is y exists'. The former may have existential
import but only the latter is an existential sentence. A logical
grammar that preserves this distinction will lack semantic explicitness, and the traditional grammar of logic allows for classes

of sentences (the *S* is *P*, some *S* is *P*) that have no existential conditions written into their syntax. In allowing this, the traditional doctrine of logical grammar is sensitive to the variety of truth conditions for sentences within a given class and insensitive to the modern requirement that a logical syntax, worthy of the name, is determined by truth conditions.

Quine is historically right in saying that Frege's conceptual script (*Begriftschrift*) was designed to achieve semantic explicitness. This motivation played no important part in Leibniz's program. Moreover, Frege himself was aware of this difference between himself and his predecessors. In a summary of his views to Darmstaedter (1919) Frege says:

> My particular conception of logic is initially characterized by the fact that I put the content of the word "true" at the beginning and let it immediately be followed by the thought with respect to which the question of truth arises. In other words, I do not begin with concepts out of which the judgment is composed but I get to the parts of the thought through the splitting [Zerfällung] of the thought. In this respect my conceptual script is different from similar creations by Leibniz and his successors in spite of its possibly misleading name [*Begriftschrift*].[6]

This passage alludes also to the primacy, in Leibniz's concept-script, of the logic of terms. For Leibniz the logic of terms was thought of as prior to propositional logic—the logic of truth functions. Thus Leibniz thought of 'if *p* then *q*' as rather like 'every (state in which) *p* is a (state in which) *q*', treating conditionals as universal categoricals whose terms are nominalized propositions and conjunctions as particular categoricals ('some [state in which] *p* is a [state in which] *q*'). Although Leibniz gave priority to terms, his notation councils neutrality. In an important series of papers Leibniz uses "coincides with" as the basic syncategorematic element which can stand between terms or propositions:

> A proposition is 'A coincides with B' where A and B can signify either terms or other propositions.[7]

In those papers Leibniz strove for, and almost achieved, a higher level of abstraction, a neutral system that would at once

6. G. Frege, Hans Hermes, Friedrich Kambartel, and Freidrich Kaulbach, eds., *Nachgelassene Schriften* (Hamburg: Felix Meiner, 1969), pp. 288f.
7. Parkinson, *Leibniz Logical Papers*, p. 55.

comprehend propositional and term logic.[8] In this respect the algebraic notation that we have developed is fully Leibnizian. For it shows us that the schemas 'every S is P' and 'if p then q' have the same for '$-x + y$'; a similar isomorphism is exemplified by 'some S is P' and 'p and q', both of which have the form '$+x + y$'. Since this is so it is a mistake to assign analytical priorities to either type of schema.

In an unpublished set of class notes aptly entitled "Leibniz's Syllogistic-Propositional Logic," Hector-Neri Castenada of the University of Indiana has called attention to Leibniz's concerted attempts to unify term and propositional logic. Castenada considers this program to be of first importance, and he is also aware of the importance of Leibniz's doctrine that singular propositions have dual quantity. The idea of a generic concept-script sufficiently abstract to represent theological structures of categorical (subject-predicate) propositions and their truth-functional compounds is original with Leibniz. So far as I know only Castenada has given adequate weight to this fundamental contribution by Leibniz to the theory of logical grammar. It is all the more important because Frege rejected it. In Frege's system every proposition is atomic or constructed out of atomic propositions by means of formative (syncategorematic) elements. Since 'every S is P' is not atomic it must be *analyzed* in terms of its atomic elements. This establishes the analytical priority of 'if Sx then Px' and with it the essential priority of 'if . . . then . . .' to 'every . . . is . . .'.

Russell once compared a notation to a live teacher. The algebraic concept-script teaches us to comprehend under one rule such seemingly different kinds of inferences as

1. $a = b$, b is p, hence a is p
2. if p then q, p, hence q
3. every S is P, whatever is Q and not S is R to some S, hence whatever is Q and not P is R to some P.

The "oppositional" (plus-minus) notation teaches that inference from more than a single premise is almost always a matter of substitution *salva veritatae:* given a premise '. . . x . . .' we may, by canceling (substitute 'y' for 'x' and), infer '. . . y . . .' in every case where '$-x + y$' is also given. The schema '$-x + y$, . . . x . . . , hence . . . y . . .' is simple and comprehensive and it forcefully illustrates the generic character of the plus-minus notation.

8. Ibid., pp. 47–89, 90–92, 93–94.

Conclusion. The algebraic transcription of regimented declarative sentences of natural language is logically useful and comprehensive. It therefore constitutes a logical syntax. The extent of a logic that uses such a formalized natural syntax is not now known, but it is much more far reaching than it is commonly thought to be. We conclude that the assumed gap between logical form and natural syntax seems bridgeable. One final remark: the representation of all logical signs as signs of opposition is a consequence of the effort to realize Leibniz's program. Beginning with the natural assignments for 'is' and 'isn't', we have been led to the view that 'every', 'or', and other logical signs can be represented by one or more signs of opposition. The implications of this simplification warrant a logical investigation that is entirely independent of the question of the alleged syntactical gap that separates formal logic and natural language.[9]

9. David Massie ("A Philosophical Essay on the Logic of Terms" [Ph.D. diss., Columbia University, 1970]) has shown the completeness of the algebra for propositional and syllogistic logic.

REFLECTIONS ON KRIPKE

David Shwayder

I have not yet seen any published commentary on Kripke's New System,[1] which promises to be most influential, and the chance to take an early shot at this material is too good to let pass. I hope I am not often off-target because of misunderstanding.

There is nothing I have read, of recent vintage, I find more persuasive or more disquieting. Much of the material is a triumph of audacious good sense, in which Kripke criticizes the right false theories and destroys the right false idols. Novel and daring positions are taken, and the right doubts are raised. The work combines a stunning simplicity of conception with a breathtaking sweep of application. Kripke's thought on myths and

1. The original occasion of this effort was an invitation to respond to a lecture Kripke was to present to the Oberlin Colloquium for 1972, as it turned out on the topic of Vacuous Names and Mythical Kinds. This talk was recorded and transcribed, but remains unprinted in this volume (see Preface). I prepared my response from an earlier version of Kripke's presentation, recorded in a seminar he had conducted at Berkeley, of which he provided me a copy. Actually, when I first accepted the Oberlin invitation I didn't know for sure what Kripke would be speaking on. I had, however, just had the profitable and pleasurable opportunity to read through an early version of his lectures on Naming and Necessity, now published in G. Harman and D. Davidson, eds., *Semantics of Natural Languages, Synthese* Library (New York: Humanities Press, 1972), pp. 253–355 with "Addenda" at 753–59. I decided to hedge against likelihoods by noting down such thoughts as I had about that work. That turned out to be well-advised, since Kripke's thoughts on Vacuous Names and Mythical Kinds are best understood as an application of the general doctrine.

What now follows is on the general doctrine and its applications. It has been redone from my notes with little additional consultation of Kripke's papers. To avoid further lengthening a presentation already too long, I have for the most part eschewed quotation and other forms of documentation, and shall assume that the reader is familiar with the broad lines of Kripke's doctrine as found in "Naming and Necessity" (hereafter N&N), and his earlier "Identity and Necessity" (hereafter I&N), in Milton K. Munitz, ed., *Identity and Individuation* (New York: New York University Press, 1971). I am grateful to my colleagues Hugh Chandler, Arthur Melnick and Robert Monk for many useful comments and criticisms, and also to a reader for the Yale University Press who found an important mistake.

fables is but one such application. His efforts here should assist
the triumph of good sense over orthodoxy, and work to correct
a nearly universal mishandling of jaded examples—unicorns have
been harnessed to bad theories and run too hard in a bad cause.

Kripke's proposals are fresh, but the inspiration is classical. I
shall draw some parallels and divergencies between his doctrine
and precedents from the history of philosophy. Concentration
on proper names, as on the problem of other minds, is a pretty
modern kind of thing—a reflection, no doubt, and a refraction,
of the traditional concern with substance—and on this Kripke
has interesting things to say; what attracts me more in his work
are his proposals concerning common names or, to put it better,
concerning sorts and stuffs. Here his efforts are part of a salu-
tary, growing movement back into more traditional territories,
somewhat neglected by philosophers since the New Departure
of Leibniz. Here also lies a danger of anachronism, especially
in appealing to logical modalities for purposes of explicating
essentials. It may be that an object has certain features just because it is the object that it is, without its necessarily having to
have any of those "essential properties." Kripke's doctrine, that
identities when true are necessary, is a bridge—a shaky one, I
believe—from the new fashion back to the old philosophy.

Kripke's theses are tightly meshed. This has created a problem,
which I have not solved to my own satisfaction, of determining
in what order to take up the parts. Let me begin with two
central issues on which I am satisfied that Kripke has made a
convincing case.

A Priori Knowledge and Necessary Truths.   Kripke tells us
that we must not confuse questions of the *a prioricity* of knowledge with questions of the *necessity* of truths. Necessary truths
may be a priori or a posteriori, and contingent truths also (if it
is proper to speak of "knowing" *truths* in this way). He suggests
by his examples, and I agree, that science at its best seeks
demonstrative a priori knowledge, formulated as necessary
truths, of facts usually first detected a posteriori. The whole
structure of Euclidean geometry in its relation to the empirical
rules of surveying used by the Egyptians is a classical example.
Einstein's demonstrations of the necessity of the Principle of
Equivalence and of the Lorentz Transformation, both previously
accepted as uncomprehended facts on the basis of delicate ex-
periments, are also possible cases in point.[2] I regret Kripke's

2. My own favorite case was Del Cano's startling, empirical discovery
of the apparent need to advance the calendar a day before completion of

occasional slippage of position in speaking of a priori truths and knowledge of necessary facts, and I suspect this may abet his rather too easy way of ascribing logical modalities to states of affairs, phenomena, facts, and the like. An important special case of the general distinction between the a priori and the necessary for Kripke's own system is his distinction between expounding the meaning of a designator, sometimes with attention to what must be so necessarily, and the a priori fixation of reference by contingent marks. I shall return to that, but for now it provides introduction to the second area of agreement.

Names are Names.   Kripke is right to insist upon the parallels between proper names of particulars (whatever particulars are) and common names of natural kinds and stuffs, for these two species of names are semantically more alike than modern practice has recognized. He is right in his resolve to concentrate on names literally taken. Yet I think he fails to hold the line here too, because he neglects other different parallels, such as that between symbols like "3" and "Au," which are *not* names literally taken. For now, let's look to what's right. The first and most important point of similarity between proper names (hereafter "p.n.'s") and common names is a negative one: the meaning of neither sort of name should be identified with any one property or cluster of properties in the named subject, or with any group of subsidiary properties attaching to instances of the named kind. It remains, on the positive side, that the referent of such a designation can be fixed a priori, by attention to the presence of properties contingently attaching to the referent or its instances and by appeal to standards, exemplars, and characteristic experiences. Kripke's observations open the way to a criticism in depth of the doctrine of the qualitative determination of individuality and/or identity best known from Leibniz's idea of a totalized "individual concept." The parallel for sorts would be the traditional quest for essences, as Locke (not Aristotle) would have conceived it, eventuating in the resolution of an idea of substance into an assemblage of "simple ideas." It follows from all this that names are not covert descriptions, either of individuals or of sorts.

Rigid Designators and Necessity.   Kripke's alternative to the position that names are covert descriptions is that they are

---

his circumnavigation of the earth from east to west. When it was recently rumored that a pair of mathematicians had found a solution to the four-color problem and this was related to an Urbana geographer, his immediate reaction was, "So, what's news?"

"rigid designators," useful and perhaps required for grounding the imaginative projection of counterfactual possibilities: we consider how things might have been for a "given" object or species. I defer consideration of this thesis about names until we have secured a surer grasp on what rigid designators are supposed to be.

Kripke's introduction of the idea seems to be tied in with a larger doctrine concerning the nature of logical necessity and possibility. He repudiates the "just look at it over there in that other place" picture of the location of possible worlds. If there ever was a case of abstraction gone crazy, that was it. Kripke instead *seems* to work with the eminently sane idea that a possible world would be exhibited by a stipulation concerning what might have happened to some actually existing thing, such as Nixon. We need never peer at anything other than what is given to hand. Possibilities exist as "suppositions" or "stipulations" made relative to the use of a "rigid designator" of a "given" object, deemed fixed across a prospective range of possibilities.

Minimally taken, Kripke's current opinion is a throwback to a position patronized by both Leibniz and Arnauld, that possibilities exist only relative to and in dependence upon an "understanding": "In order to call anything possible it is enough that we are able to form a notion of it when it is only in the divine understanding, which is, so to speak, the region of possible realities."[3] But for "pure possibilities" Leibniz demanded a "divine understanding" capable of comprehending all possibilities in a completely unconditioned, utterly global sort of way.[4] It seems that all Kripke wants is an object to hand, conceptually fixed in some one or other rigidly designative way. This is an entirely natural view long ago espoused by Arnauld in his criticism of Leibniz's *individual concepts*. What Kripke says about this rigidly designated ordinary thing—Nixon and Elizabeth II are his examples—almost echoes Arnauld's words about that object which Arnauld rigidly designated as "Moi." I quote at length:

> Moreover, Monsieur, I do not see how, in taking Adam as an example of a unitary nature, several possible Adams can be thought of. It is as though I should conceive of several possible me's; a thing which is certainly inconceivable. For I am not

3. Gottfried Wilhelm von Leibniz, *Discourse on Metaphysics, Correspondence With Arnauld, and Monadology*, trans. George R. Montgomery (La Salle, Ill.: The Open Court Publishing Company, 1902), p. 131.
4. Ibid., p. 119.

able to think of myself without considering myself as a unitary nature, a nature so completely distinguished from every other existent or possible being that I am as little able to conceive of several me's as to think of a circle all of whose diameters are not equal. The reason is that these various me's are different, one from the other, else there would not be several of them. There would have to be, therefore, one of these me's which would not be me, an evident contradiction.

Permit me, therefore, Monsieur, to transfer to this me what you say concerning Adam and you may judge for yourself if it will hold. Among possible beings God has found in his ideas several me's of which one has for its predicates, to have several children and to be a physician, and another to live a life of celibacy and to be a Theologian. God, having decided to create the latter, or the present me, includes in its individual concept the living a life of celibacy and the being a Theologian while the former would have involved in its individual concept being married and being a physician. Is it not clear that there would be no sense in such statements, because, since my present me is necessarily of a certain individual nature, which is the same thing as having a certain individual concept, it will be as impossible to conceive of contradictory predicates in the individual concept me, as to conceive of a me different from me? Therefore we must conclude, it seems to me, that since it is impossible for me not to always remain myself whether I marry or whether I live a life of celibacy, the individual concept of my me has involved neither the one nor the other of those two states. Just as we might say that this block of marble is the same whether it be in repose or in a state of movement and therefore neither movement nor repose are involved in its individual concept. This is why, Monsieur, it seems to me, that I ought to regard as involved in my individual concept only what is of such a nature that I would no longer be myself if it were not in me, while, on the other hand, everything which is of such a nature that it might either happen to me or not happen to me without my ceasing to be myself, should not be considered as involved in my individual concept (although, by the ordinance of God's providence, which never changes the nature of things, it could never happen that that should be in me). This is my thought, which, I believe, conforms wholly to what has always been held by all the philosophers in the world. . . .[5]

5. Ibid., pp. 94f.

Without however stopping over that which I have already said, namely, that taking Adam for an example of a unitary nature it is as little possible to conceive of several Adams as to conceive of several me's, I acknowledge in good faith that I have no idea of substances purely possible, that is to say, which God will never create. I am inclined to think that these are chimeras which we construct and that whatever we call possible substances, pure possibilities are nothing else than the omnipotence of God who, being a pure act, does not allow of there being a possibility in him. Possibilities, however, may be conceived of in the natures which he has created, for not being of the same essence throughout, they are necessarily composites of power and action. I can therefore think of them as possibilities. I can also do the same with an infinity of modifications which are within the power of these created natures, such as are the thoughts of intelligent beings, and the forms of extended substance. But I am very much mistaken if there is any one who will venture to say that he has an idea of a possible substance as pure possibility. As for myself, I am convinced that, although there is so much talk of these substances which are pure possibilities, they are, nevertheless, always conceived of only under the idea of some one of those which God has actually created.[6]

6. Ibid., pp. 96f. Here is still another quotation from Arnauld: "Now I find in myself the concept of an individual nature since I find there the concept *me*. I have, therefore, only to consult it in order to know what is involved in this individual concept, just as I have only to consult the specific concept of a sphere to know what is involved there. Now I have no other rule in this respect except to consider whether the properties are of such a character that a sphere would no longer be a sphere if it did not have them; such, for instance, as having all the points of its circumference equally distant from the center. Or to consider whether the properties do not affect its being a sphere, as for instance, having a diameter of only one foot while another sphere might have ten, another a hundred. I judge by this that the former is involved in the specific concept of a sphere while the latter, which was the having a greater or smaller diameter, is not at all involved in it.

"The same principle I apply to the individual concept me. I am certain that, inasmuch as I think, I am myself. But I am able to think that I will make a certain journey or that I will not, being perfectly assured that neither the one nor the other will prevent me from being myself. I maintain very decidedly that neither the one nor the other is involved in the individual concept me. 'God however has foreseen,' it will be said, 'that you will make this journey.' Granted. 'It is therefore indubitable that you will make it.' I grant that also. But does that alter anything in the certitude which I have that whether I make it or do not make it I shall always be myself? I must, therefore, conclude that neither the one nor the other enters into my *me*, that is to say, into my individual concept. It is here

Both Kripke and Arnauld are exercised to resist the resolution of identity into qualitative determinations. Both writers seem to hold that possibilities are to be conceived relative to some one or other thing that could not be anything other than it is. I suppose that the latter condition can be satisfied only if the object is selected by way of a certain kind of reference—Arnauld's token reflexive "me" or what Kripke more generally calls a "rigid designator," and which he explains as an expression which designates the same object in all possible worlds. A rigidly designative reference (if I may put it that way) selects an object with reference to which various possibilities may be conceived.

If we allow Kripke his thesis that p.n.'s are rigid designators, this consequence, also implicit in Arnauld's remarks, seems to follow, and I quote: "an identity statement between names [*sic*], when true at all, is necessarily true, even though one may not know it a priori."[7]

The argument is almost instantaneous. If N_1 and N_2 rigidly designate n, then N_1 and N_2 both designate the same object, n, for all possible worlds, and the statement $N_1 = N_2$ is true for all possible worlds; hence the statement of identity "between" these is necessarily true. That argument applies just in cases where both expressions' claims to be a rigid designator are sustained.

That is not the end of the matter, however. It seemed to me that what started out to be a theory of p.n.'s in Lecture II of N&N turned into a general theory of identity in Lecture III, and I felt the same transition even more strongly in I&N. Kripke appears to maintain that *all* true statements of identity are necessary: "identity is not a relation which can hold contingently between objects."[8] We are not originally confined to equations formulated with rigid designators; rather, the converse thesis, that a "proper" equation must be formulated with rigid designators only, seems to be what we have in hand. Why should that be so? Kripke tells us that a true identity asserts that an object is the same as itself. We proceed to reason that, since any object must be identical with itself, it follows that what a true statement of identity asserts must be true; hence every true statement of identity is necessarily true. Unsurprisingly, Kripke also holds to the converse thesis that true inequations are necessary.[9]

---

it seems to me that we must remain without having recourse to God's knowledge, in order to find out what the individual concept of each thing involves" (ibid., pp. 98f.).

7. N&N, p. 310.
8. N&N, p. 341.
9. For which see N&N, n. 56.

If this is indeed his view, I find difficulty in it. First, there is a suggestion of sophistry here. Why, by Kripke's argument, shouldn't a false statement of identity also be necessarily true, since a false no less than a true statement of identity asserts that an object is the same as itself? I suppose Kripke would reply that a false statement of identity asserts that one object is the same as another. There is an ambiguity in that formula. A statement of brotherhood asserts that two objects are brothers. That could be read to mean, first, what is impossible, that I might assert that two cousins are brothers or, second, what is quite possible, that I assert of two cousins that they are brothers. The formula about identity must surely be taken in the second way, that I assert of an object that it is the same as itself. Taken in this sense, the formula, when applied to false statements of identity, yields a nearly unsayable thought to the effect that I say of two objects that it is the same as itself.[10] It probably makes sense, however, and I suppose Kripke would find his way round this first obstruction, thus resolved, by simply observing that we could not detach the conclusion which states necessity if the antecedent were false.

Second, contingently existing things are snags. Such objects, though they do exist, might not have, and so they do not exist in some "possible world." Following what we have already reviewed, we would presumably conceive these possibilities relative to other rigidly designated objects. Suppose we have two (existing) distinct and hence necessarily distinct objects: these might not have existed in different "counterfactual circumstances," hence in different "possible worlds" relative to each other. I do not see how to represent this relationship within Kripke's revised modal logic. I run into the following kind of problem. Bodies are presumable contingently existing particulars. I assume that they are "individuated" in the largest connected regions they completely occupy at times. If a body moves from R_1, t_1, where it gets called "a", into R_2, t_2, where it gets called "b", then $a = b$. Let us suppose that at t_2, b spontaneously splits into separated and distinct bodies, b_1 and b_2, and that b_2 almost immediately disintegrates. In those circumstances I would want to say that a was identical with b_1. However, it might have been b_1 instead of b_2 that disintegrated, in which case a would have been identical with b_2 ($\neq b_1$). Kripke says that if $a = b_1$, then that would be so in all circumstances in which a (and b_1?) existed: $a = b_1 \supset \square \exists x \cdot x = a \supset a = b_1$.[11]

10. Cf. I assert of one object that they are brothers.
11. N&N, p. 311.

But I have suggested that we might want to say that, although $a = b_1$, we can imagine that a would have been b_2, where b_1 and b_2 are actually if transiently existing distinct bodies. There is a suspicion in all this that no contingently existing object, hence (presumably) no material body can be rigidly designated or identified in any way; if so, there goes the application to actual proper names like "Kripke." ("Strongly rigid" numerical designators like "5" and "$\sqrt{25}$" are Kripke's preferred illustrative specimens of rigid designators in I&N.)

I am not sure how far Kripke wants to go with the necessity of identity, and I'd like to consider this a bit. In his lectures on Naming and Necessity he seems to allow that true statements of identity involving descriptive references may be and usually are only contingently true.[12] That brought me up against a wall. First, if Kripke accepts Russell's analysis of descriptions, then an equation formulated as ⌜The ϕ = The ψ⌝ must be read as stating that there exists an object which is uniquely ϕ and which is uniquely ψ. Is that a statement of identity? Perhaps Kripke would be pleased if it weren't. Still, we have an identity function under the quantifiers here; more seriously, a quantifier would sometimes have to reach to the identity function through a modal operator, if Kripke's thesis is to admit of coherent formulation $[(x,y) : x = y \supset \Box\, (x = y)]$ and therewith disputes about "quantifying in." I do not see how to explain the sense of the identity function to gain Kripke's position. To stipulate in advance that all singular terms are either rigid designators or descriptions, where, of these, only the former can occur in genuine statements of identity, would perhaps yield the wanted conclusion that all true substitution instances of the function are necessarily true, but only at cost of begging the main question at issue. I can't believe that Kripke would go for a substitutional analysis of quantification strongly confined to the substitution of rigid designators.[13] His own words are that free variables can be used as rigid designators of unspecified objects.[14] I really don't know what that means—doesn't the designator specify the object?

The Contingency of Existence. Kripke says that if $a = b$, then $a = b$ in all circumstances in which we can imagine a to exist, and in that qualified way, $a = b$ necessarily. The existence of a could be a matter of contingent fact. Kripke says that when he uses "the notion of a rigid designator, I do not imply

12. E.g., N&N, p. 334.
13. See, e.g., N&N, p. 310.
14. N&N, n. 16.

that the object referred to necessarily exists,"[15] even though he maintains that existence taken as a property is trivially necessary to anything that exists.[16] One might wonder whether Kripke can reconcile the contingency of existence with the necessity of identity. Consider: if an object exists then it exists in all circumstances conceived relative to itself, hence necessarily in relation to those possibilities. Hence all actually existing objects exist necessarily. Leibniz argued in somewhat that way against Arnauld's statement that purely possible substances are chimeras and that "we conceive nothing as possible excepting through the ideas which are actually found in the things which God has created." To this Leibniz replied, "If we wish to reject absolutely the pure possibles, contingencies will be destroyed, because if nothing is possible except what God has actually created then what God has actually created would be necessary in case he resolved to create anything."[17] He invoked a distinction between absolute, metaphysical necessities of which the truths of geometry are instances and hypothetical necessities which have a "relation to the existence of things and to time."[18] Contingent truths, he seemed to hold, are necessities contingent on existence. Of this, a special case would be

(NI) $a = b \supset : \exists x \cdot x = a \supset \square (a = b)$.

That thesis, following modern principles, quickly leads to the conclusion that nothing exists except necessarily.[19]

---

15. I&N, p. 146.
16. I&N, n. 11.
17. Leibniz, *Correspondence With Arnauld*, pp. 116, 131.
18. Ibid., p. 106.
19. Logic supplies the "modern principles" to which I add that *a exists* is equivalent to $\exists x \cdot x = a$, that truths of logic are necessary (T) and the distribution of $\square$ over $\supset$, $\square (p \supset q) : \supset : \square p \supset \square q$ (D), all of which I find doubtful.

(1) $b = a \cdot \supset \cdot \exists x \cdot x = a$ Existential Generalization and Conditionalization
(2) $\square (b = a \cdot \supset \cdot \exists x \cdot x = a)$ (T)
(3) $\square (a = a \cdot \supset \cdot \exists x \cdot x = a)$ Substitution of "a" for "b"
(4) $\square (a = a) \cdot \supset \cdot \square \exists x \cdot x = a$ Conditionalization and (D)
(5) $\exists x \cdot x = a \& a = a \cdot \supset \cdot \square (a = a)$ Substitution of "a" for "b" into (NI) and Importation
(6) $\exists x \cdot x = a \cdot \supset \cdot \square \exists x \cdot x = a$ Syllogism applied to (4) and (5) and Elimination of Tautologies

(The fact that we could have gotten the more striking conclusion $\square \exists x \cdot x$

Kripke's thesis is $a = b \supset \Box \, (\exists x \cdot x = a \supset a = b)$, not NI. But he sometime talks as if he would subscribe to that too. The conclusion is a *Tractarian* conception of necessarily existing basic particulars which can be imaginatively assembled into various *Sachverhalte*. There is at least one place where Kripke seems to endorse the principle of reducing facts to basic particulars.[20] We shall also see that Kripke holds that if Homer, the traditional author of the *Iliad* and the *Odyssey*, did not exist, he couldn't have.

Kripke's Essentialism.   Kripke is peripatetic in the modern style of holding (or seeming to hold) that a property is essential to an object if and only if the property attaches to the object necessarily.[21] This use of the logical modalities is alien to the classical tradition. A more general idea of essential property broad enough to cover both the classical and contemporary notions may be prosaically explained either in terms of existence or in terms of identity. An essential property of an object is a property that object has either just because it exists or just because it is the object that it is. Kripke puts it both ways, and argues that they come to the same: "What are its essential properties? What properties, aside from trivial ones like self-identity, are such that this object has to have them if it exists at all, are such that if an object did not have it, it would not be this object?"[22] I have a method of separating considerations of existence from considerations of identity, but that is a story for another day. Since I prefer the explanation in terms of identity and since that seems acceptable to Kripke too, let's adopt it. What does it mean to say that an object has a property just because it is the object that it is? As a sufficient condition: if $a = b$ entails Fa, then F is essential to a; if $\Box \, (a = b \supset Fa)$, F is essential to a. Given this condition, it does not follow by ordinary logic alone that an essential property of an object holds of the object necessarily ($\Box \, Fa$). However, if we allow Kripke his thesis of noncontingent identities and assume that $\Box$ distributes over $\supset$, then it would indeed follow that a property essential to an existent holds of it necessarily. Here is that shaky bridge I mentioned between the classical and the modern doctrines.

= a from (4) without the intervention of (NI), by simple appeal to the necessity of $a = a$, shows that we had better not assume any such thing when "a" stands in for a vacuous name.)

20. N&N, p. 271.
21. N&N, n. 12.
22. I&N, pp. 151f. with n. 12.

In the classical tradition, the essential property par excellence of any object was for the object to be of its species. Fido is essentially a dog. Everything else that contributes to the formal principle of the substance is swept in. That is not my view, but Kripke seems to go along.[23] He seems to believe that Descartes was nothing if not a person.[24] Again: *a pain* surely is the sort of thing a pain is; Kripke declares that he finds it "self evidently absurd" to assert that (what happens to be?) a pain existed yet was not (always?) a pain.[25] Being a pain, he says, is the most obvious necessary property of a pain, and he argues from the premise that a pain is nothing if not felt.[26] I have my doubts, since I find good sense in a roused sleeper's remark that he must have been wakened by the stomach ache he now feels. A classical thesis, for the most part conformable to "ordinary language" but extremely hard to rationalize, from which the conclusion naturally flows, is that there is exactly one thing every substance can be truly said to be in itself, such as a dog or a human being. Most partisans of species-essentialism also adhere to the thesis, recently advocated by Geach and opposed by Quine, that identification is always species-relative. Speaking for myself, I think that the metamorphosis of *an* object is possible; for example, an ovum becomes a fetus or a block of wood a table. Perhaps Kripke would allow that and wish to maintain only the more modest position that, for instance, Descartes was essentially a *sometime* human being. (He does seem to pin essence to timeless properties,[27] but I'm not sure what that means for him.) A plausibility problem remains. Suppose the table I used when I just wrote down these notes— give it the proper name "T"—was hewn from a block of wood that we may denominate "W". I suppose that by Kripke's theory $T = W$ necessarily.[28] But now, since T is essentially a table—that is what it is in itself—T is essentially something which was (sometime) designed to have things put on it. It seems to follow that W—our original block of wood—is (was?) essentially something which was (sometime) designed to have things put on it. That is counter-intuitive.

Kripke seems to make two substantial additions to classical

23. See N&N, n. 57, where he includes even species of artifacts, such as tables.
24. N&N, pp. 334f.
25. I&N, p. 162, n. 17.
26. N&N, pp. 335, 339.
27. N&N, n. 57.
28. See N&N, p. 314.

species-essentialism. First, I think, he throws in the times and places of origin of bodies. Second, he wishes to include the material constitution of bodies, presumably localized to space and time.

The first seems right to me, at least if we don't equate essentials with necessities. A body could be identified from its origin, hence its being in that place at that time would be among its essential features. But then all other time-places along the body's world-line should also be included.

Material constitution brings in other considerations. Kripke concentrates on composition at time of origin,[29] but he also suggests that being made of wood was an essential property of his lectern at the time of one of his lectures.[30] I think that it is not merely the kind of stuff but the actual quantity of stuff from which the body is made that Kripke has in mind, and he does use *hunks* of matter.[31] So being made of that stuff from which a body is made at a given time and place seems to be a Kripkean essential feature of the body. Why should that be so? Bodies and quantities of stuff are identified in different ways, for bodies may change with respect to the stuff they are made of and quantities of stuff be redistributed among different bodies. Bodies and the quantities of stuff they are made of are differently identified. However, the body and the quantity of stuff it is made of at any given time are individuated together. From this I think it follows that if there is a body in R at t, then necessarily the smallest body occupying the whole of R at t equals the body constituted of the smallest quantity of stuff occupying the whole of R at t (from which it does not follow by ordinary logic that the body was necessarily thus constituted).

Kripke's two additions are un-Aristotelian. Material constitution and space and time are, in Aristotle's scheme, tied in, not with the formal principle, but rather with the material principle that sets one individual off from another. However, if essential species determinations are also to be localized to space and time, as I have suggested Kripke may wish to hold, the Aristotelian distinction between *form* and *matter* may disappear from his scheme.

Predicables of Necessity. Kripke believes that if a predicable F holds of an object necessarily, then another predicable of

29. N&N, p. 314.
30. I&N, p. 152.
31. At n. 56 of N&N. The latter would include the former if we also go for Aristotelian essentialism, since the stuff-kind is the species of the stuff.

being necessarily *F* also holds of the object. He characterizes
the latter item as a property "involving modal operators."[32]
I believe the invocation of such things is gratuitous, obscurantist,
and probably mistaken.

Kripke seems to need modal predicables to formulate certain
alleged "truths" such as $(x,y) \cdot x = y \supset \Box (x = y)$. I should
think that anything one can get from that formula could be
more cleanly procured from a schematic rule of inference $A = B, \dashv \Box A = B$. I daresay he would not agree with that, for he
declares that the formula in question "does not say anything
about *statements* at all. It says for every *object x* and *object y*,
if *x* and *y* are the same object, then it is necessary that *x* and *y*
are the same object."[33] He goes on to argue that *being necessarily x* is, by Leibniz's Law, one of the properties anything
equal to *x* must have. I think that it is perverse because it
blatantly involves obscure and disputed notions.

What kind of complex predicable is a □*F*? It's not like *being
big and juicy*. Suppose when Secretariat is entered in a race, all
the other horses that were to run are scratched because their
owners fear humiliation for them. We can say that if Secretariat
is a winner, he is a necessary winner. I suspect that is like being
an alleged winner or a likely winner. Kripke probably believes
it is more like running second, which is a predicable easily
represented with quantifiers. Yet it can't be quite like that,
since, unlike any bank of quantifiers (for example "[∃x] [y] "),
"□" can in Kripke's usage apply to functions of arbitrary
complexity, because it must have that capacity from its role
as a statement operator.

Kripke's free way with necessity simply leaves the large question of when we can and cannot quantify-in unresolved. That
there is an issue is clear even from the example of the essential
predicables of blocks of wood which are tables. A block of
wood is essentially something which is designed to have things
put on it only qua (when referred to as a) table, or something
like that.

It seems to me, in any case, that statement operators cannot
always be transformed into predicate-components. I say, "This
pencil is here." My reference to the pencil is secured by the
fact that the pencil is here, and what I refer to as "this pencil"
could not now be elsewhere. But surely no one is going to conclude from that ascription of necessity that my pencil has the
property of being necessarily here.

32. I&N, p. 137.
33. I&N, p. 137.

Many will suspect that Kripke's predicates of necessity are conceptual pretenders disguised in formal regalia.[34] That naturally leads to a still larger question.

What Is Necessary?   Kripke lays a great burden of necessity upon his readers. Truths—statements, propositions, assertions, sentences or other things of that ilk—are sometimes made subject to modal operators. But not they alone. We have seen that he sometimes insists upon incorporating modal operators into predicates with the result that objects—bodies, perhaps— are asserted to be necessarily something. It doesn't stop there. He freely speaks of necessary *facts*, *states of affairs*, and *phenomena*, and he means it. The necessity asserted in a truth of identity attaches not only to the produced statement—that an object referred to in one way is the same as an object referred to in another way—but to the fact of identity itself. The need for necessary facts or phenomena appears at every point in his defense of dualism. We are directed to suppose that "Descartes" and "B" are rigid designators of Descartes and his body, respectively; he then argues that, since *Descartes* = *B* if true is necessary, Descartes could not exist without *B* and *B* could not exist without Descartes.

I have a sense of being fooled by mirrors. A standard objection to the one argument is that the same body under some other description needn't have been Descartes. Kripke acknowledges this by poking fun at it. But there is a large philosophical issue at stake, over whether only *thinking*, *saying*, *meaning*, and the like can be strictly said to be either necessary or contingent, or whether *facts* also qualify. Behold Kripke! The statement produced in saying that this thing is identical with itself seems on the face of it to be different from the statement that *Saul* = *Kripke;* but it is at least arguable that the asserted facts are the same. So is the fact necessary in both formulations? Consider the three statements:

1. "Kripke is before us."
2. "Saul is before us."
3. "Our first speaker is before us."

34. He appeals to the intuitions of ordinary men against the preconceptions of philosophers (N&N, p. 265). This domestic note rings out of tune with the highly theoretical character of the *logical* modalities, little used even by our pre-Leibnizian philosophical forebears. In my judgement, the "mays" and "mights" of daily life formulate what Kripke calls "epistemic modalities." One holds back from asserting that John is not there by saying, "He may be there," because one does not know that John is not there.

Here the "same thing" is said, in each case about the same
object, and these very different statements are "made true" by
the very same fact, that this object (Kripke, our first speaker)
is before us. But then it seems no different with *Saul = Kripke*
and *Our first speaker = Kripke.* Here too we have the same
fact twice formulated, once in an allegedly necessary statement
and then again in a clearly contingent one. This is the kind of
argument that has led many of us to think that facts, unlike
truths, are never properly said to be either necessary or contingent. Of course that is only one view of the matter; Kripke's
theory offers another.

Russell collapsed the distinction between fact and proposition, and Kripke's theory may be a throwback to Russell's.
According to that theory,

1. The meaning of a "logically proper name" (read "rigid
   designator") is the object meant.
2. That object is a "constituent" of propositions asserted
   by use of the name.
3. True propositions are facts and the meanings of logically
   proper names, therefore, may also be constituents of facts.
4. Every assertion of a proposition in ultimate analysis is a
   proposed relating of meant objects; the proposition is fact
   if the meant objects are related as proposed.

How does this work for identity? What fact is asserted? I
think it can only be the fact of the exhibited object, namely
that object which is and can be identical only with itself.

I won't say that this is all wrong; but I certainly do not feel
that it is all right, either. It leads naturally to the *Tractarian*
demand for necessarily existing basic particulars.

On the Meaning of Names.   I now turn to some "semantics"
in a sense that may interest linguists. When Kripke tells us that
names are rigid designators, he means names literally taken,
including proper names of persons, cities, and countries,[35]
common names of species of things and stuffs, and perhaps
abstract nouns like "yellowness" for good measure.[36] I haven't
been able to come to a settled opinion on whether he is right
about names being rigid designators. At this time of final re-
writing, I am inclined to think he is, but with qualifications
and reservations. He also says other things about names, to

35. N&N, p. 254.
36. N&N, n. 66.

which I'll add my bit, concentrating in this section and the next on p.n.'s.

I have already expressed my complete agreement with him that names literally taken—how else?—do not mean any one property or several properties of their referents, and are not synonymous with (almost any) co-referential descriptions mentioning such properties.[37] That notably applies to descriptions of the form "the object called NN."

So what is the "meaning of a name"? I'm not sure what Kripke means by the "meaning of a name." At one point,[38] in citing Ziff as one "who explicitly [denies] that names have meaning at all even more strongly than I would," he suggests that names don't have meaning. But presumably there is something like meaning which stands to names as meaning stands to "serendipity." In Lecture I of N&N, where Kripke argues that p.n.'s are not descriptions on the grounds that the named referent might not have had the describing feature, I got the impression that he thought that the meaning of a name, in a reduced sense of "meaning," must have something to do with necessity. But later on, in Lecture III, he seems more concerned with telling us what names *are*, semantically speaking, and here he notably refrains from appealing to the essentials of the referent as factors contributing to the meaning of its designators.[39]

The most important thing Kripke has to say about the meaning of names, as we now may understand the matter, is that names are rigid designators. That does not entail that the rigidly designated referent of a p.n. is any part of that name's meaning, and I doubt that Kripke intends that it should be. While his metaphysics may be Russellian, his semantics is not.[40]

37. "Almost any," except for ones which themselves involve identity, e.g., *being identical with Kripke,* as in "The man who is Kripke is the man who is Saul." This use of the identity function may give what he calls a "trivial fulfillment." (N&N, n. 38.) I think this exception should cause Kripke some pause in his orthodox treatment of identity as a relational predicable.

I doubt, by the way, that Frege should be placed in the opposition, and apparently so does Kripke sometimes (see N&N, n. 22). A *Sinn* might be almost anything "meant" that could lead us to the *Bedeutung* of an expression. I take it that a *Sinn* is an indication of what information should be used in order to locate a referent and to determine the truth values of sentences in which reference is made to those referents.

38. N&N, p. 259.

39. See especially N&N, n. 58.

40. I once thought that Kripke believed that the referent was the most important part of its meaning. Against that, he never, in my recollection,

Second, Kripke seems to hold that it is always part of the meaning of a name that we can "fix the reference" (better, "the referent") by use of a description, such as "our first speaker" or "the man they all call 'Saul'." He denies that these referent-fixing properties contribute anything to the meaning of the name.

Third, the meaning of a p.n. is determined by a "causal chain," winding back through a community of speakers, to—what? I think he wants to say, to an act of naming or calling, or baptizing, or assuming, or something of that order. An act of naming, for instance, links the chain to the ground—to its referent. That is the kind of "ostension" I think Kripke could approve of for investing names with meaning.[41] I take it from this that Kripke would say it is part of the meaning of a p.n. that it is or would be given by an act of naming, or calling, or something similar. Note well, however, that this differs from the opinion that names are synonymous, in whole or in part, with descriptions like "the person who was given the name NN on occasion O." This appeal to naming is not circular because we may take it that a name is available to be given and used; names are words that can be "given" in this way, and that is a feature of their meaning. It is a part of the meaning of a p.n. that objects can be so called, as would be well understood by one who learns from a dictionary that "Ivan" is the Russian Christian p.n. corresponding to "John." That part of the meaning of a name does not change as we move from one so-called referent to another.

So, in summary, Kripke holds that a name is a rigid designator which can be given by an act of naming, where designees can be fixed by description.

When I first read Kripke's work, I was beset with misgivings, now diminished, by a sense that something *more* had to be said about names. I felt this partly because there are many kinds of names—Christian and other names, family names, nicknames,

---

even so much as suggests that "light" and "stream of photons" have any part of their meanings in common, though he does think that they rigidly designate the same phenomenon. Furthermore, if the designated object were any part of the meaning of a name, then a reference-fixing description would give at least some of that meaning, which Kripke denies. The named referent need be no more part of the meaning of a name than any (other) essential feature of that object.

41. See, e.g., N&N, pp. 298f. *Giving a name* is, I think, what Kripke must have in mind when, on one occasion, he speaks of "primitive reference." (N&N, n. 43.)

diminutives, sobriquets, acronyms: "Saul," "Kripke," "Saul
Kripke," "The Stagirite," "Africanus," "William I," "The
Conqueror," "The Bastard," "UNESCO," "TWA." These would
presumably be classified according to *meaning*. But also, there
are other singular terms, doubtless rigid designators in Kripke's
lexicon, which are not names literally construed, and they too
must have distinctive kinds of meaning. I think chiefly of
symbols like "3," "π," and "Au," in contrast with the name
"the Lorentz Transformation." I think Kripke would say that
a *description* like "the largest even number that does not satisfy
Goldbach's Conjecture," if it designates anything, is a rigid
designator. Of course, the other things Kripke tells us about
names may make the distinction between names and descriptions.

Kripke's admittedly "pictorial" way of speaking of "causal
chains" in connection with the meaning of p.n.'s, as it stands,
seems to me to be as useless as it is vague. In company with
Mill and Russell, Kripke seems to picture names as something
like what my colleague Melnick aptly calls "long distance
demonstratives," indicatings made away from the spot. I sit
here writing out "Julius Caesar" with my right hand, all the
while with my left hand figuratively gripping the right hand
of another, on back through the chain until we finally get to a
person who has his left hand on Julius Caesar's shoulder. But
of course "long distance demonstrative" is a contradiction in
terms; it is always part of the meaning of a demonstrative
that its occurence should indicate that one is to utilize materials
at hand to select a referent. Is it then that the meaning of the
name is in the chain and not in the demonstration? Perhaps;
but then we need to be specific about the chain, for not any
old chain anchored in any old act of naming will do: matrimonial
renamings commonly issue in a nonsemantic posterity. What
is a semantic posterity? Surely the contingencies of transmission
are pretty incidental to the sense of a name. It can't matter
to my use of "Julius Caesar" whether I first came upon that
name in reading about him or from the lips of a junior high
school Latin teacher. What must matter here is, first, the
peculiarities of the linguistic kind of communication by which
the use of the name is conveyed and, second, the peculiarities
of the "calling" by which the name is linked to its referent.
Kripke says next to nothing about either of these matters. He
rightly refuses to pin everything to any one particular kind
of name-giving or calling. Yet surely the details of this must

matter to the meaning of any particular name. Among the many different ideas at work here—all of them are important and too much neglected by philosophers of language—are *naming, calling, referring, addressing,* and *announcing.* All of them may be done with *some* names like "Saul," but surely not with all names. Raleigh, for example, might have addressed Elizabeth Tudor as "Majesty," which was not one of her names, and *referred to* her as "the Queen," by which title she might be *announced* but not *addressed.* With regard to causal chains, I sense that a great deal more must be said before this picture can be seen to have any pertinence at all to the meaning of a p.n.

I would start with the thought that a *proper* name is a singular term by which speakers are enabled to indicate the existence of individuals and hence to refer to those individuals. It is part of the meaning of (most) p.n.'s that speakers may use them to mean different referents: "Saul was named king by Samuel" and "Saul was visiting at Berkeley last term (Spring, 1972)". This way of putting the matter turns upon a distinction between what words mean and what speakers mean. It is a feature of *the* (the one) meaning of many words that they enable speakers to mean different things. Thus it is a feature of the meaning of "this" that it enables speakers to mean an object at hand. It is specifically part of *the* meaning of a p.n. that speakers should be able to use it to mean different "given" objects—one Saul or another.

This same distinction between name-meaning and speaker-meaning and the relationship between them is important for the mechanism by which the use of a p.n. is causally conveyed from one speaker to another. Each successive speaker may ask his predecessor, "Whom do you mean?", and the predecessor must be able to "fix" the reference à la Kripke in terms of properties the meant referent sometime had. The successor may go on to find out something else about referent, and at the next stage of the transition he may use that information to "fix" the reference. I ask Plutarch who Julius Caesar was, and am told perhaps that he was the illustrious Roman who vanquished Pompey on the field of Pharsala and was assassinated on the Ides of March; I later find out that he came, saw, and conquered somewhere out in Turkey and authored the *Gallic Wars;* and perhaps that is what I tell my nephew when he asks me. Now this tale comes to nothing unless it is understood that different speakers may mean different properties of the intended referent, and that *that* semantic potential should be part of the meaning of a p.n. It is furthermore implied that the meant properties are ones the object came to have on some occasion in the course of its career. The referent could have been identified on every such occasion, not merely verbally but, so to speak, materially. Thus, at every link in the chain by which the name is conveyed, different properties of the referent are brought into play, and, furthermore, different links are added onto an implicitly indicated parallel chain of identifications of the referent—from the time he was first called Julius, to Gaul and back, and thence to the field of Pharsala and back to the senate steps on the Ides of March. The crucial part of this picture of the meaning of a p.n. is that it is always part of that meaning that it enables different speakers to mean different properties of an identifiable referent. However, such speakers, when merely using the name and not conveying it, do not normally say what they mean. To say that the referent is fixed by some feature known by the speaker which the speaker means when he uses the name and that this capability should be part of the meaning of a name by no means implies that any of the speaker-meant features are "connoted" or otherwise meant by the name itself. For these reasons, it is always permissible for an interlocutor to ask the speaker, "Who d'ya mean?", and the speaker should be able to give an answer of the "$\phi-\psi$" form: "I wonder where Christine is now." "Who?" "You know, the guy who had himself made over into a woman." Such an exchange does not supply a paraphrase of the name; it is an amplification or clarification of what the speaker meant. It thus appears that it is always part of the meaning of a p.n. that different speakers may use that name in the self-same sense to refer to the self-same referent, and mean different things. Thus, in speaking of "Saul," Kripke's mother may mean "my son the mathematical philosopher", and I "that fellow who published a Completeness Theorem for Modal Logic in the *JSL* way back in 1959." But the meaning of "Saul" stays put.

Finally, names are given as names; and so, following Kripke, part of the meaning of a name always is to enable speakers to indicate that the referent was so named in a specific manner on an occasion from which subsequent identifications could have proceeded. Thus, a *prénom* is officially given, a surname is taken after the name of a family, a patronymic after the father's *prénom*, a nickname is given by a familiar, and so on.

We now have quick answers to the questions posed earlier.

First, different kinds of names are gained by different kinds of namings. Second, the causal chains by which names are transmitted are semantically limited by the consideration that each speaker along the way should be able to fix the reference in terms of some feature the referent sometime had, and this is warranted by the consideration that it is always part of the meaning of a p.n. that different speakers might mean different such reference-fixing properties. The chain along which the name is conveyed from speaker to speaker implies the existence of a parallel chain of identifications on occasions upon which the referent came to have the various meant properties. One expects further restrictions upon the kind of properties that can be meant by the use of any particular name: one who understands the use of a p.n. like "Christine" knows it is a female person, just as anyone who understands the use of "Hibernia" or "Iberia" or "Albion" knows that they are countries.[42]

Third, p.n.'s are distinguished from demonstratives in that it is no part of the meaning of demonstratives that speakers should use them to mean any one or another of the properties of the meant object at hand. Proper names are furthermore distinguished from other rigid singular designators of "given" objects of the mathematical-symbol sort, in that it is no part of the meaning of these latter that writers using them mean possibly different identifying properties: anyone who knows the full meaning of "3" must know that 3 is the third natural number.

Finally, we have a solution to the ancient problem of conceiving the inexistence of properly named things which can be conceived of only as existing. We suppose that the description which gives the properties by which the speaker knew the referent was not satisfied, without relinquishing the principle that the property is no part of the meaning of the name.

Let me add in passing that we have now spotted part of what makes the cluster picture beguiling. The amorphous and undelimited assemblage of properties that may cluster together, while certainly in themselves no part of the meaning of the name, are brought into play as properties speakers may mean in using the name in its own proper sense. The friends of clusters misplace these properties in their picture due to failure to distinguish what a word means from what people may mean by using the word in that meaning.

42. With tedious qualifications: dogs and hurricanes are, by transferred usage, also given personal names.

What we still have not done is to provide explication of what it means to say that names are used to refer to "given" objects. That belongs with the question of whether names are rigid designators, to which I now proceed.

Are Proper Names Rigid Designators?   I can well imagine someone saying, "If Shwayder were Kripke, he would have an answer to that question." Let that criticism pass, for it may be only a funny way of saying that Kripke has the answer. I don't; but I do have some ideas. I don't think Kripke's thesis commits him to regarding p.n.'s in the literal sense as "logically proper names" in Russell's sense. Still there is that question of whether properly named, contingently existing bodies can be rigidly designated. That Julius Caesar ≠ Augustus Caesar is, I believe, a truth of history. Suppose Julius had had no sister; then (by Kripke's analysis) his grandnephew Augustus would never have been. So Augustus does not exist in one of Julius's possible worlds, and I find the question whether they would be distinct in such circumstances mystifying, to say the least. I suppose Kripke would say that they would be distinct on condition that they both existed.

What about identical twins, which originate from a single ovum and a single sperm? Romulus and Remus are distinct. If their dividing cells had not got disconnected into separate embryos, as we may well imagine, would Romulus have been Remus, or would Kripke say that neither twin could have existed in such circumstances?

It is a truth of history that Augustus Caesar was Julius Caesar's grandnephew Octavian. So presumably Octavian = Augustus. Is that necessarily true? Well, Octavian was so called sometime before the Battle of Actium and received the name "Augustus" upon his investiture by the Roman Senate. Careful historians observe this order of events in their choice of name. The chains of identifications underlying these names are linked to different occasions. Any causal connection between the two is, I suppose, contingent in the sense that there is some sequence of true contingent statements relating the events in question. That consideration would cut no ice with Kripke, who could simply reply that the man who came to be called "Augustus" was in fact Octavian, and *that* person could not have been anyone else. I find this very hard to counter.

What most inclines me to think that Kripke is right about p.n.'s being rigid designators is that p.n.'s are pre-eminently employable to make reference to "given" objects: the object is "given" by name. Not all rigid designators have that feature; but it may be that all designators which have that feature are rigid. What is a "given" object? My first inclination was to say something mysterious: a reference to a *given* subject identifies a subject *as* an identified subject. Mere identification is not enough, as comes out in the examples

1. "That is our first speaker."
2. "That is Saul Kripke."

"That," while perhaps "rigid"—any other subject would be a different "that"—selects a subject but does not identify it.[43] "Our first speaker" does identify a subject, but somehow does not refer to a "given" object, presumably because it doesn't tell us who that subject is. But "Saul Kripke," it seems, both identifies a subject and tells us who it is.

My own picture of the situation is this. An "identifying reference," such as might be conveyed by a definite description, fixes a "point" through which various "world lines" can be drawn, representing different possibilities. That point might be joined to *This* or *That*.[44] Now my account of p.n.'s secures that any speaker's use of a name implicitly determines at least *two* points: one is associated with the place and time upon which the referent came to have the identifying property meant but not said by the speaker, and the other with the place and time of naming. "Two distinct points determine a unique line," which in my picture represents a unique sequence of identifications from the occasion of naming to an occasion of identification upon which the referent could have been observed to have the property meant by speaker. Each such occasion includes a region in which the body in question could have been "individuated" at the time in question, and every identification in the sequence takes us from one such "individuation" to a succeeding one. The "meant" line of identifications at once represents an unspecified stretch in the actual career of referent and provides a "basis" from which possible prolongations of its career may be conceived. So the "given" referent, as

43. "This = This" if true must be, and "This ≠ That" if true must be. Of course these things are never said, because the rule of necessity here precludes speech. I wonder why "This = Saul Kripke" if true shouldn't be necessarily true in Kripke's account.

44. *This* could of course be joined to differing places at other times but not to another currently indicated *This* or *That*.

represented by the line of identifications, is common to all
these "possible worlds" conceived relative to it as prolongations.
   One might make the point less figuratively in this way. The
use of a body-referring p.n. implies the possibility of identifying
a body from one meant occasion to another. There can be only
one sequence of identifications from the one occasion to the
other—otherwise questions about identity lapse. Now suppose
the object is given a name on one occasion and then another
name on another. Of course, the object needn't have come to
be called by either name. But speakers use those names to mean
the object that did come to be called by those names on those
occasions of naming. We use "Augustus" to mean the man
who came to be so called upon the occasion of his investiture;
and now I agree with Kripke that he couldn't have been anyone
else. A person who truly says "Octavian = Augustus" links
those occasions. Put otherwise: In saying "Octavian = Augustus,"
the speaker at once indicates that he means the man who came
to be called "Augustus" and who satisfies the referent-fixing
description, "the man who had previously been known as
'Octavian'." "Augustus" provides one basis, "Octavian" another;
if the equation "between" them is false, the two lines stand
disconnected; if it is true, and we know that, we have extended
our basis, and neither segment of it can be used to disqualify
the other. All sorts of things could have happened to Augustus
from the time he came to be called "Octavian" to the time of
his investiture. Furthermore—and here is where I think I disagree with Kripke—the extended basis could be variously "pro-
longed" from either end into different possible lines of identification. The upshot seems to be that what is meant by any
speaker making correct and knowing use of an equation "between" p.n.'s, if true at all, is true in all circumstances conceived relative to the referent "given" in either way. Every
such speaker, however, knows that other such speakers may
mean other bases for identification and, furthermore, all such
speakers may suppose that the intended referent could be otherwise identified in alternative ways. So, while equations "between" p.n.'s express propositions which if true and known are
necessarily true, it does not yet follow that identity cannot be
a "contingent relation" between objects.
   I am groping here, but also grappling with something which I
think does issue from my description of the meaning of proper
names. It gives me greater appreciation for Kripke's thesis that

p.n.'s are rigid designators. However, I do not think the conclusion carries over to species names, to which I now turn.

Names of Sorts and Stuffs.[45]   What Kripke has to say about "gold" and other names of stuffs and about "tiger" and other names of natural kinds almost parallels what he says about p.n.'s of particulars. He makes equally severe criticisms of the cluster concept analysis of both, and I think he holds that both sorts of names are "rigid designators."[46] His observations about sorts and stuffs are sometimes reminiscent of what Locke had to say on the same topic, and both are dealing with questions first raised by Aristotle. A quick comparison may be useful for getting things started.

All three writers agree, and I agree too, that sorts exist if and only if instances do. It would seem to follow from this that all these writers are committed to a distinction between the "meanings" of predicates and the sorts those predicates are used to name. Thus Kripke, casually and by the way, indicates a distinction between the species *cow* and the predicable *being a cow.*[47] Aristotle recognized the need for some such distinction in the *Posterior Analytics,* and what he had to say about it is most instructive indeed. First, "we cannot apprehend a thing's definable form without knowing that it exists, since while we are ignorant whether something exists we cannot know its essential nature"; and again, "whoever knows what a man is, or what anything else is, must also know that it exists, for no one knows the nature of what does not exist."[48] The modern reader would ask how in the world anyone could know that a man or a goat-stag existed if one did not know what a man or a goat-stag was. To this Aristotle would have responded, "One can know the meaning of a phrase or a name if for example I said 'goat-stag', but it is impossible to know what a goat-stag is."[49] So Aristotle would surely have allowed that we can know

45. The important differences between sorts and stuffs do not affect what follows. Kripke's treatment of natural kinds—which are sorts—resembles Locke's treatment of substances, and both of them take *gold* as a guiding case. Stuffs are more productive illustrations because the chemists have given us much more to work with than have the naturalists.

46. I am uncertain about whether he means to include all common names and mass-nouns or only some, and about whether he has in mind all sorts or only a restricted class of natural kinds (substances or species). So, for example, I don't know whether "the king of the beasts" is for Kripke an acceptable name, or whether *the lioness* is an acceptable sort.

47. N&N, p. 322.

48. Aristotle *Posterior Analytics* 93a. 19.

49. Ibid., 92b. 6.

the meaning of a predicate—specified as what some of his com-
mentators call a "nominal essence," "a set of words which
signifies what some name signifies"—before considering whether
anything of the species named by the predicate exists at all and
before undertaking any scientific inquiry into essences. But
then the named species and the meaning of the name are not
the same.

Going on from that, all three writers seem agreed that substances (natural kinds) have "archetypical" instances. Furthermore, we commonly come to know what those sorts are by
examining such instances for their properties. The reference to
the sort can be "fixed" by attention to the presence of such
properties.

However, Kripke and Locke agree, and I agree too, that no
cluster of properties turned up in the course of such an investigation defines the sort. We cannot define the sort by any list
of "characteristical" subordinate properties. Not all that glitters
is gold, and not all that is gold is yellow necessarily, even though
we might direct attention to what we mean by gold by fastening
upon its golden color. Any list of subordinate properties provides at best what Locke disparaged as a "nominal essence."
His explanation of the defects of such definitions is like the
familiar explanation of why we cannot determine individuality
in purely qualitative terms. In both cases, our "ideas" are "inadequate" to their instances. I believe the Kripke would agree.[50]

"Real essences"—a different matter altogether—are conceivable
though seldom attained. A knowledge of these, Locke held,
though first gained a posteriori by way of a scientific investigation into the minute parts of things, if sustained by reason,
would qualify as "certain knowledge" of relations of ideas,
formulable in necessary truths. Kripke surely would agree with
that, and also with Aristotle that natural kinds have essential
generic properties. Locke contemned the quest for that kind of
essence.

For present purposes, Kripke's most important departure

50. Kripke does not expressly indicate that he would go along with
one way in which Locke expounds the relation between a sort and the
subordinate properties of its instances. Locke was prone to say that
different people would explain what they differently mean by *gold* by
mentioning different subordinate properties; but he usually avoided the
conclusion that "gold" has many different meanings. (See, e.g., *Essay*
III.vi.31.) This corresponds to my proposal about proper names, that it
is part of the meaning of a p.n. that different people may mean different
properties with that name used in that meaning.

from the doctrines of our predecessors is that he apparently
does not countenance a distinction, upon which Aristotle,
Locke, and I too would insist, between what Locke called *substances* and *mixed modes.* My evidence for this is Kripke's denial,
for which he promises but does not produce a justification, that
there are two concepts of metal—a phenomenological and a
scientific one.[51] This distinction is central to my own way of
thinking about these matters, and also to my criticism of Kripke.

Not surprisingly, Kripke's main thesis about sorts and stuffs
concerns identity, now what he calls "Type-Type" identity,
identity of sorts or stuffs. One could hold, as in fact I do, that
all persons are sometime live human bodies, and the converse,
without holding (as I do not) that the sort *person* = the sort
sometime live human body. Kripke's favorite example is the
identity of gold with chemical element #79. A case, interesting
for its complications, that concerns species is that of the yeti.
Tracks were sighted—at least they looked like tracks. Sceptical
westerners would presumably fix a reference to the yeti, if it
exists, as the creature who left the tracks. Of course, that is not
what the yeti *is.* Suppose Dryenfurth runs him down and dis-
covers (as some believe) that the yeti is a bear. Call it *Ursus
Himalayensis.* Presumably he would have shown that the yeti
is (=) *Ursus Himalayensis.* Kripke holds that the statement that
gold = element #79 if true is necessarily true; and I guess he
would hold the same opinion about our imagined case of the
yeti. He doesn't say whether he thinks that all such true statements are necessarily true, but I guess that he would. (The statement that *gold* = *the world's most hoarded metal,* while contingent, is not of the right form.)

Kripke's line in regard to sorts and stuffs designated by common nouns and mass-nouns runs parallel to his line regarding
properly-named particulars. Similar perhaps manageable difficulties appear in the considerations that named species which do
exist might not have, and distinct species might by some quirk
have evolved independently into a single species. There is,
however, an important difference. The terms in the statements
of particular identity were proper-name references of much the
same sort, for example "Octavian" or "Augustus." But Kripke's
preferred examples for sorts are identities that incorporate
scientific designations on the one side and popular designations
on the other. I initially found Kripke's thesis about sort and
stuff identities counterintuitive, perhaps because my intuitions

51. N&N, p. 315.

had been corrupted by the influence of Locke's distinction, rejected by Kripke, between substances and mixed modes. (I take mixed modes in the sense of *Essay* III.v.1, as *species*, and not in the sense of II. 22, as mere ideas.) That, of course, touches the point of difference. Gold is (like) a substance, while #79 is a mixed mode. Since sorts and stuffs may be either mixed modes or substances, but not both, it would follow by Leibniz's Law that gold ≠ element #79. That argument, however, simply begs the question against Kripke.

My first attempts to resolve the issue without relying upon Locke's distinction left me in a state of confused indecision, more friendly toward Kripke's thesis, but not so friendly as to let it go unchallenged. I came back to Locke in this way. Since we may have identity of class over distinctness in sorts, why then not also have distinct sorts with necessarily coextensive memberships? Cases of this could be set in useful contrast with cases where sortal identity is not in doubt. A case entirely acceptable to me but too much in dispute for purposes of argument is that of the human person and the human body. How about the twentieth-century Gregorian leap year and the twentieth-century American election year? Each year of the first sort is a year of the second, and conversely; I am inclined to think that this is so necessarily, yet surely these are different year-sorts. The first was ordained by Gregory XIII, but not the second; whereas the second, but not the first, was indirectly provided for by the United States Constitution. If it be thought that the determination of election years reposes too much on mere contingent circumstances, what about Kripke's own mentioned but undiscussed case of the statistical mechanical and thermo-dynamic notions of temperature or the notions of inertial and gravitational mass? Or this: Call exponents for which the equation of Fermat's Conjecture do not hold "non-Fermatian Powers." It may be that this sort of number is necessarily coextensive with the even primes; but the number-sorts in question seem distinct. In contrast with these cases, it seems to me unquestionably true and necessary that element #79 = the element represented as *Ib-3* in the Periodic Table.

My intuition gets a better grip on questions of sort and stuff identity precisely where only what I would classify as mixed modes are involved. I have almost no intuitions about substance identity. With mixed modes, schemes of calculation are provided. We get to #79 and to Ib-3 by running through the same table by different paths to arrive at the same position. In contrast,

we calculate Gregorian leap years by a rule almost entirely
unrelated to that by which we calculate American election
years. But in both cases we work with stipulations lacking for
substances but of the essence for modes.

Barring identities achieved by mere verbal stipulation such
as those by which English German Shepherds patriotically
become Alsatians or Wittins Windsors, the question arises
whether anyone who allowed for a distinction between substances and modes could admit *any* cases of substantial identity.
I think they cannot. As I see the matter, questions about identity
of sorts arise primarily and most fundamentally in relation to
instances: we hold up two things and ask, "Is this the same
sort of thing as that?" The decision could be made only with
an eye to subordinate properties and relations. Thus we distinguish a horse from a mule by the shape of the ears, or size,
or because we find a jackass on the escutcheon. But Locke and
Kripke have taught us that that won't do in general. These
features are accidental to the sort, and, of course, one observer's
distinction is another's irrelevancy. Recent work in evolutionary
genetics confirms our sense that natural species smudge. Substances, like gusts of wind and real numbers, have no discrete
and proper identity; they can be prospectively distinguished
perhaps but not identified. It will certainly be different with
the mixed modes that will someday be contrived to supplement
the substances of daily life. Ticking off chromosomes and saying
how they are assembled from nucleic acids will perhaps someday
do for natural kinds what physics has already done for gold
and other stuffs.

I have been sneaking through an indirect argument for the
validity of something like Locke's distinction between substances and modes. It can be supported by "category arguments"
after the fact. We say, "Water usually contains dissolved minerals," or "Pure gold is too soft for door locks." But it makes
only doubtful sense to speak of H_2O containing dissolved
minerals, for H_2O is just that molecule and no other; and it
makes only doubtful sense to say that Au (= #79) is pure or
impure, since it is the scientific standard for the purest gold.
We shall, perhaps, some day wish to say that one DNA molecule
sired another, but surely not in just that sense in which donkeys
sire mules.

I now hope to have supplied protection against Kripke's con-
tempt for Locke's distinction between substances and modes.
But its main vindication will come in application. (It will be
put to work in my later discussion of myths and fables.)

Even if modes and substances are always distinct, they do sometimes "correspond," and the question arises over what style of correspondence this is. My rather uncertain impression about this presupposes a distinction. Now, a sort exists if and only if an instance does. The best opinion is that the yeti, which would be a substance if it did exist, in fact does not. I have been told that the best opinion is that chemical elements after #126—and these are modes—neither do nor can exist. So here there is no difference between modes and substances. Such differences as there are can, I think, be best brought out by concentrating attention on the distinctive ways in which our conceptions—what Locke called our "ideas"—of substances and modes are employed in reference to their instances, which may be, and perhaps even necessarily are in some cases, the same. Locke was apt to put this by saying that our ideas of modes are "made by the mind." That is not yet very useful, if only because there is a sense in which all our conceptions can be said to be "mind-made." It is more pertinent to observe that our ideas of substance are adjusted to their instances, whereas instances of modes are trimmed and judged for their degree of approximation to the ideal. We adjust our idea of what a dog is to the dogs we meet; in contrast, geneticists may someday be able to tell whether this is a canine chromosome by seeing whether or to what degree it meets specifications still undrawn. Substances are fitted *onto* their instances and the instances are fitted *into* the mode. A substance is essentially what we find it to be, whereas a mode is essentially what we say it is. Our ideas of substance are "responsible" to (at least some of) their instances in ways in which our ideas of modes are not.

It would seem from this that substances, if they exist at all, have "archetypical" instances. That is not so for modes. Their instances are invariably in some degree "impure." The demand for paradigms for substances having ordinary common names corresponds to the requirement that the referent of an ordinary proper name must have sometime been so named.

By way of compensation, modes have *specifications*, whereas substances do not. So, for example, one gives the specifications for a *machine* or a *molecule;* but there is no end to what one might say by way of explaining what he thinks a dog is.

We have now found a new formulation for that point on which Locke and Kripke are agreed, that natural kinds or substances cannot be defined in terms of any one or cluster of subordinate properties attaching to their instances: substances do not and cannot have specifications. We begin (or "fix the reference") with an observation of archetypes, and there is no limit to what might be noticed and taken to be characteristic of the kind. Any selection would be only one out of any number, and to that extent at best accidental, suitable only as a merely "nominal essence."

In our use of modes, however, we are free from the controlling influence of instances; we can specify their "essence" as it were, by fiat. This secures a (revisable) restriction upon what is deemed "relevant." For example, the possibility of compass slippage is irrelevant to the conception of a circle, but not to the conception of an ellipse. As Locke put it, the nominal and real essences of modes coincide.

It turns out then that the doctrine of nominal essence and Kripke's criticism of qualitative reduction are consequences of the principle that our ideas of substances are "inadequate," that is, they are inadequate to their archetypes, just as proper-name references are "inadequate" to their referents. (This "inadequacy" is semantically displayed in the consideration that it is always part of the meanings of both proper names for whatever and common names for natural kinds that different speakers may use those names in those meanings to mean different subordinate properties.) Names of modes (often cast as symbols) are to substance names rather what symbols like "3," "π," and numerical designations of persons are to p.n.'s.

Just as the army and the IRS find it convenient, perhaps even necessary, to eschew personal designations in favor of numerical ones, so the progress of science characteristically eventuates in the supplementation of substances with modes. Taxonomic science achieves this at a rather low level; chemistry, physics, and economics do so more impressively. Strict standards are thus imposed upon the phenomena, and features of personal interest are swept aside as irrelevant. The specifications of supplementing modes are deemed to give the real essences of the supplemented substances. Now it is a Principle of Bureaucracy that every numerical designation should correspond to some named victim; ultimately, it is Tavis McTaggart who is taxed to pay for the drafting of Llewelyn Jones. Similarly, if substantial instances couldn't be fitted into modes, these modes would be a scientific waste of time, frivolities. So here is our "correspondence." The mode is vindicated only if the fitting in is pretty often pretty good. The mode becomes a standard for the substance, not in the way in which the standard meter is standard, for it is only one archetype among many, but rather

in the way that arithmetic provides a standard for the arithmetical combination of aggregates. Something like this lies under
our idea that a substance and its correspondents are necessarily
coextensive.

Our distinction between modes and substances, clearly, is not
a distinction among "things"; it is a distinction among sorts,
what Kripke calls "types." If anyone protests that it is not
even a distinction among sorts but only among concepts or
"ideas," I must reply that what I have said goes some way
toward explaining why *modes* can be effectively distinguished
and identified and *substances* cannot. If that is correct, then
we must finally allow for a difference between p.n.'s of identifiable particulars and common names of substantial sorts, trace-
able to a "categorial difference" between essentially indiscrete
sorts and identifiable bodies. There is a "criterion of identity"
applicable to bodies, however these bodies are referred to, by
which it can be shown that #521 28 2461 = D. S. Shwayder;
that statement may even be necessarily true. However, if substantial sorts are not identifiable at all, any identification of a
substance with a mode must be defective.

Fictions and Fables.   Kripke wants to deal with fictions as
part of a general attack on vacuous names. I don't think that is
the only way in, and it risks leaving us in the wrong room.[52]   In
quick summary, here are what I take to be Kripke's conclusions.
First, questions about the existence of Hamlet, Holmes and
unicorns are not questions about whether a description or a
story is true of something or other. I agree with this. Second,
no person *could* be Hamlet and no animal *could* be a unicorn
or a chimera: Hamlet *could not* have existed as a person or
unicorns as animals. Again, I agree; unicorns are nothing if not
fabulous and chimeras are essentially chimerical.[53]   Kripke also
wants to say, as part of his second thesis, that if Homer did not

52. There are at least three issues here, for which Russell provided a
single resolution. Philosophy still hasn't completely recovered from this
sweeping use of the theory of descriptions. The first issue has to do with
the possibility of assertions and denials of singular existence. The second,
to which we now proceed, has to do with the names of fictions. The third
has to do with the "status" of names which happen to have no referents
and with the status of assertions enacted with such names. Kripke,
mistakenly, I shall argue, attacks this third issue along the lines by which
he finds a correct resolution for the second.

53. I first came to this conclusion from a remark of Austin's about the
Loch Ness monster. When a sighting was reported, some responded, "So
you see there is a monster after all," and others, "So you see there really
wasn't any monster there at all."

exist, he couldn't have, and if yetis don't, they can't. (Homer
is his example; the yeti is mine.) I disagree with that.

What is the alternative to Russell's theory of descriptions for
handling "Hamlet" and "unicorn"? Kripke calls them "fictional
names" and he once said that Hamlet and unicorns are referred
to "fictionally." That is ambiguous. It could mean that "Hamlet"
is the name of something which could exist as a fiction or that
"Hamlet" is not really a name at all but rather a pretended
name. Kripke in fact is careful to separate questions over how
these seeming names work in a story—Homer's, Shakespeare's
or ours—from how they work in games of charades, crossword
puzzling, literary criticism, and like frivolous activities. In
literary criticism, these words are used as names of fictions,
which may or may not exist: thus Zeus's spouse (= Hera) existed
as a creature of Greek mythology, whereas Artemis's husband
didn't; Hamlet did, Gonzago did not. My only contribution
to this matter is to suggest that fictions are "modes," not "substances." Otherwise, I agree with Kripke's line on these things,
and they needn't detain us. Kripke concentrated on the first
context, on Shakespeare's use of "Hamlet," and rightly so, for
it does come first.

So in regard to the use of seeming names in relating fictions,
Kripke tells us that these are not really names at all, but rather
pretended names, and that the storyteller is not asserting
propositions but, rather, pretending to do so. What one in this
style pretends to assert are not propositions (pretended or otherwise). What is then said in fictions does not raise possibilities.
"There is no counterfactual situation properly described as
being one in which there would have been unicorns." I have
amended this to read that no *animal* could be a unicorn. Kripke
argues, first, that since "the myth provides insufficient information about their internal structure to determine a unique species,
then there is no actual or possible species of which we can say
that it would have been a species of unicorns."[54] To this he
appends an "epistemological argument" roughly to the effect
that, since unicorns are mythological contrivances, we could
not trace an historical connection to show that unicorn-like
creatures, should they be found, are the subject of the myth.
The causal chains for pretended names are secured, not by acts
of naming, but by Big Lies. But then they are pretended *names*,
introduced under the *pretense* that conditions for giving a
name were satisfied.

54. N&N, p. 761.

I agree with this entirely. It does, of course, raise questions over what these acts of pretended assertion achieved by use of pretended names are. Since Kripke does not dwell on this, neither will I.

Kripke also wants to say something similar about "Homer" and (I guess) about "the yeti," and other seeming names of *legendary* and *reputed* things: if the legendary character did not exist, the name is fictitious. The difference is too great to be handled in that way. The yeti may exist as an animal (what else?). I have my doubts, yet it may be so. Should one turn up to match the supposed tracks, it may be a primate or a bear or even a reptile, for all I know. We can be sure, however, that it will have to be some such thing or other, and have loads of other features too. The yeti, if it exists, is a "substance," not a "mode." Again, it seems to me that "Homer wrote the Iliad" has a different "status" from "Poseidon favored the Achaeans." My use of "Poseidon" and "unicorn" are knowingly borrowed from the story, but my use of "Homer" from a long tradition of reputed authorship. Observe also, in Kripkean vein, that such yetis as there may be might not have the features of which the Sherpa legends speak. Legends, such as that of Homer and St. Philomena, unlike myths, such as that of Poseidon, are supposed to have existed as animals, and if it appears that they did not, people may be sorry. For example, the recent extrusion of Philomena from the Roman calendar has compromised the good name of numerous parochial schools, and may have caused regrets among their alumni.

In maintaining that if Homer did not exist, "Homer" is a pretended name, otherwise a real one, Kripke needlessly mars his account of fictions by mistaking ignorance for pretense. One's sense of disappointment at this needn't owe to a stubborn adherence to the position that whether a term has reference cannot depend on contingent fact. Suppose that some Ionian lover of myths felt certain in his bones that his two favorite epics were authored by the same man, whom he called "Homer." This gives a name, *if* Homer existed. Does it not give a name if there was no Homer, if, for instance the two epics were separately authored by identical twins? I can accept that. Still our myth lover didn't lie or pretend, and so Kripke couldn't trace "Homer's" causal chain back to an act of that kind. It really does, we suppose, go back to an act of naming, which might, however, have failed to come off. Perhaps "Homer" fails as a name. But do we really want to hold that a faulted act of naming is a

successful act of pretended naming? Not I. Nor do I want to
say that a faulted name is a pretended one. My way of looking
at the matter immediately leads to a familiar analysis of reference
failure for names in acts of assertion: the use of faulted names
issues in faulted assertions, perfectly meaningful no doubt but
unsuccessful in failing to produce statements, true or false,
capable of providing answers to questions whether something
was so—was Homer really blind?

PROPOSITIONS

Robert Stalnaker

Propositions are things people express when they make predictions or promises, give orders or advice. They are also things people doubt, assume, believe to be very likely, and hope are true. What kind of thing are they? My aim is to present and discuss an account of propositions that appears to have great theoretical promise, but that also is faced with serious philosophical difficulties. I will first give a brief outline of the account I have in mind; then provide this account with some philosophical justification by tying it to an independently plausible account of propositional attitudes; and finally, raise and respond to some of the serious philosophical problems that the account faces. I cannot solve them, but I hope to indicate that they are not insurmountable problems and so are not reasons to reject the account out of hand.

The account of propositions that I have in mind is a byproduct of the semantical treatment of modal logic which defines necessity and possibility in terms of a structure of *possible worlds*. According to this kind of interpretation, the formulas of modal logic are assigned truth values not directly, but relative to possible worlds or possible states of the world. Exactly one possible world, or possible state of the world, is *actual*, and truth itself is just truth in this actual world.

Just as a domain of individuals must be specified in order to interpret sentences in first-order extensional logic, so a domain of possible worlds, each with its domain of individuals, must be specified in order to interpret first-order modal logic. This move allows for a natural interpretation of statements of necessity: "it is necessary that P" means that P is true in all possible worlds in the domain. It also allows for a natural distinction between the intensions and the extensions of singular terms, predicates, and sentences. The extension of an expression is given relative to a possible world; it is what is denoted by that expression in that possible world. The intension of an expression is the rule by which the extension is determined. Thus since the extension or denotation of a singular term is an individual, the intension is a function from possible worlds into individuals (an individual concept). Since the extension of a one-place predicate is a class of individuals, the intension of a predicate—the property it expresses—is a function from possible worlds into classes of individuals. And if one takes the extension of a sentence to be a truth value, then the intension of a sentence—the *proposition* it expresses—will be a function taking possible worlds into truth values. Equivalently, a proposition may be thought of as a set of possible worlds: the set of worlds in which the sentence expressing the proposition denotes the value true.

Intuitively, this account of propositions suggests that to *understand* what a sentence says is to know in what kinds of situations it would be true and in what kinds it would be false, or to know the rule for determining the truth value of what was said, given the facts. It also means that two sentences express the same proposition in a given context relative to a set of possible worlds just in case they are true together and false together in each of those possible worlds.

Now if propositions are to be the objects of speech acts and propositional attitudes, why should they be understood in this way? Part of the justification requested by this question can be given by pointing to the technical success of the theory of possible worlds in resolving paradoxes concerning referential opacity, in finding and analyzing subtle scope ambiguities, and in providing a formally elegant framework for the representation of the structure of intensional concepts. But a more general philosophical justification for this account can, I believe, be given. This justification rests on an assumption shared by some philosophers who reject the possible-world approach, and it has, I think, independent plausibility.

The assumption is that beliefs, presumptions, and presuppositions, as well as wants, hopes, and desires, are functional states of a rational agent. A functional state is a state which is defined or individuated by its role in determining the behavior of the object said to be in the state. In the case of propositional-attitude concepts, the objects are rational agents, and the relevant kind of behavior is rational behavior. Thus the notions of believing, wanting, and intending, on the assumption I am making, belong to a theory of rationality—a theory which is intended to explain how rational creatures operate when they deliberate, investigate, and communicate; that is, to answer questions about why their actions and reactions are appropriate when they are. A simple theory of this kind goes back at least to Aristotle and is taken for granted by common sense explanations of behavior. Its most basic concepts are belief and desire (where desire is taken broadly to include long-range dispassionate ends as well as attitudes more naturally called desires). To explain why a person did something, we show that by doing it, he could satisfy his desires in a world in which his beliefs are true. For example, I explain why Sam is turning cartwheels on the front lawn by pointing out that he wants to impress Alice and believes that Alice will be impressed if he turns cartwheels on the front lawn. The notions of belief and desire used in the explanation are correlative dispositions that jointly determine action.

Now if what is *essential* to belief is that it plays this kind of role in determining action, what is essential to the objects of belief? I shall argue that what is essential is given by the possible-world account of propositions sketched above.

First, the functional account, as a theory of rational action, already contains implicitly an intuitive notion of alternative possible courses of events. The picture of a rational agent deliberating is a picture of a man who considers various alternative possible futures, knowing that the one to become actual depends in part on his choice of action. The function of desire is simply to divide these alternative courses of events into the ones to be sought and the ones to be avoided, or in more sophisticated versions of the theory, to provide an ordering or measure of the alternative possibilities with respect to their desirability. The function of belief is simply to determine which are the relevant alternative possible situations, or in more sophisticated versions of the theory, to rank them with respect to their probability under various conditions of becoming actual.

If this is right, then the identity conditions for the objects of desire and belief are correctly determined by the possible-world account of propositions. That is, two sentences P and Q express the same proposition from the point of view of the possible-world theory if and only if a belief or desire that P necessarily functions exactly like a belief or desire that Q in the determination of any rational action. Suppose P and Q express the same proposition in the sense that they are true together and false together in all possible courses of events conceivable to some agent. If any of his attitudes toward the content of P were to differ from his attitudes toward the content of Q, then no coherent division or ranking of the alternative possibilities would be determined, and no straightforward rational explanation of any action could be given. An attitude toward P will be functionally equivalent to the same attitude toward Q, and in a functional theory, functional equivalents should be identified.

Now suppose that P and Q express different propositions in the sense that there is some possible course of events in which they differ in truth value. Then one can always imagine a coherent context of deliberation—one in which the agent's attitudes toward the possibilities that distinguish the two propositions are crucial. In such a context, he will have different attitudes toward P than he has toward Q.

A second reason that the possible-world theory provides a concept of propositions which is appropriate for the functional account of propositional attitudes is that it defines propositions independently of language. If desires and beliefs are to be understood in terms of their role in the rational determination of action, then their objects have nothing essential to do with language. It is conceivable (whether or not it is true) that there are rational creatures who have beliefs and desires, but who do not use language, and who have no internal representations of their attitudes which have a linguistic form. I think this is true of many animals—even some rather stupid ones—but there might be clearer cases. Imagine that we discovered living creatures— perhaps on some other planet—who did not communicate, but whose behavior was predicatble, for the most part, on the hypothesis that they engaged in highly sophisticated theoretical deliberation. Imagine further that we had this indirect evidence supporting our hypothesis: that the beliefs that our hypothesis attributed to these creatures could be causally explained, in many cases, in terms of their sensory inputs; and that the desires attributed to them by the hypothesis were correlated appropriately, for the most part, with the physical requirements for their survival. Finally, imagine that we test the hypothesis by manipulating the environments of these creatures, say by feeding them misleading "evidence" and by satisfying or frustrating some of their alleged desires. If they continued to behave as predicted, I think we would be tempted to attribute to these creatures not just belief and desire analogues, but beliefs and desires themselves. We would not, however, have any reason to hypothesize that they thought in a mental language, or in any language at all.

It is plausible to think that if such creatures were intelligent and adaptable enough, it would almost certainly be in their interest, and within their power, to develop ways of communicat-

ing their beliefs and desires. Hence, a community of such sophisticated but inarticulate rational agents would be surprising.
But it is not an incoherent hypothesis that there are such creatures, and in any case, on the functional account, the development and use of language is viewed as one pattern of rational
behavior among others, and not as something on which the
concept of rational behavior is itself dependent. For this reason
an account of propositions that treats them as linguistic items
of some kind would be inappropriate.

Even if we are concerned only with the behavior of real,
language-using rational creatures, we should not treat the objects
of propositional attitudes as essentially linguistic. There is no
reason, according to the functional theory, a person cannot
have a belief that goes beyond the expressive power of the
language he speaks or that can be expressed only imperfectly
in his language. For example, I may believe of a certain person
I saw last week that he is a spy. I may not know his name, or
even remember that I saw him last week; I just remember *him*,
and I believe that he is a spy. You may attribute the belief to
me (for example, by saying, "Stalnaker believes that Ortcott is
a spy") in the course of explaining my behavior toward Ortcott
without attributing to me either the language in which you
express my belief or any translation of it. It should be clear that
I may have the belief even if I know of no name or accurate
unique description of the person whom my belief concerns.
But it would be gratuitous to suppose that in this case there
is a private inexpressible name which occurs in my belief. Such
a supposition would be required by an account which treated
propositions as linguistic things.

There are, of course, several essential features of the objects
of propositional attitudes which are also essential features of
linguistic items such as statements. Both can be true and false,
and can stand in logical relations like implication, independence,
and incompatibility. The possible-world account attributes these
logical features to propositions without any of the extraneous
structure of language. Propositions, according to this account,
have no syntax, no "exact words" or word order, no subjects,
predicates, or adverbial phrases; nor do they contain semantical
analogues to these notions. This accords with the functional
account, which assigns no role to such grammatical notions in
the explanation of behavior. It also accords with intuitive ideas
about belief and other propositional attitudes. We do naturally
talk about true and false, incompatible and independent beliefs.

But we do not normally talk about the first word, or the sub-ordinate clause in a belief. For these reasons, it seems plausible to maintain that while beliefs resemble statements in some ways and are often expressible in statements, they are not, as statements are, composed of linguistic elements.

Before looking at the problems with this account that I find difficult, let me dismiss two that I think are not. First, some people find that the possible-world theory troubles their ontological consciences. Since there really are no such things as possible worlds, how can we take seriously a theory that says there are? Second—a closely related worry—some people claim not to understand the notion of a possible world. They say it has no useful intuitive content, and so it cannot play an essential role in an adequate explanation of propositional attitudes.

The first objection seems to me not to be distinct from a general objection that the theory as a whole is not fruitful. If the possible-world theory is useful in clarifying relationships among actions and attitudes, or among the contents of statements and beliefs, and if the basic notions of that theory cannot be analyzed away, then we have as good a reason as we could want for saying that possible worlds *do* exist, at least insofar as it is a consequence of the theory that they do. A simple denial of existence is not a good reason to reject a theory. Rather, one has reason to deny the existence of some alleged theoretical entity only if one has independent reason to reject the theory.

Philosophers with strict ontological scruples often justify their skepticism about some alleged entity by claiming not to understand it. Some people claim just not to know what a possible world could be, not to be able to recognize one or tell that one is different from another. One aim of drawing the connection between the possible-world theory and the functional account of propositional attitudes is to help such people understand possible worlds—to support the claim that the notion does have intuitive content, and to identify one of its sources. The connection suggests that we need at least a rudimentary notion of alternative possible situations in order to understand such notions as belief and rational deliberation. If this is right, then a notion of possible worlds is deeply involved in our ordinary ways of regarding some of our most familiar experiences.

This intuitive notion of an alternative possible state of affairs or course of events is a very abstract, unstructured one, but that is as it should be. The notion of rationality, as explained by the functional theory, involves a notion of alternative possibilities, but it does not impose any structure on those possibilities. That is, it is no part of the idea of rational deliberation that the agent regard the possible outcomes of his available alternative actions in any particular way. The kind of structure attributed to possible worlds will depend on the application of the theory to a particular kind of rational agent in a particular kind of context.

While the possible-world theory itself is neutral with respect to the form of individual possible worlds, one philosophical application of the theory is as a framework for the articulation of metaphysical theories which may impose some structure on them. One may think of possible worlds as quantities of some undifferentiated matter distributed in alternative ways in a single space–time continuum, or as alternative sets of concrete particular substances dressed in full sets of properties, or as a structure of platonic universals participating together in alternative ways. Those whose inclinations are antimetaphysical may think of possible worlds simply as representations of alternative states of some limited subject matter relevant to some specific deliberation, inquiry, or discussion.

I have not really answered either the ontological skeptic or the philosopher who does not understand what possible worlds are. Rather, I have suggested that these people present not specific objections, but expressions of general skepticism about whether the theory of possible worlds has any fruitful application. A full answer can be given only by developing the theory and by applying it to particular problems.

Let me go on to a more specific and troublesome problem with the possible-world theory as applied to propositional attitudes. The problem is this: if two statements are logically equivalent, then no matter how complex a procedure is necessary to show them equivalent, they express the same proposition. Hence, if propositions are the objects of propositional attitudes, then any set of attitudes which an agent has toward the content of the one statement must be the same as the set of attitudes which he has toward the content of the other. But this is not plausible. If a person does not realize that two statements must have the same truth value, he may believe what the one says while disbelieving what the other says. And in many cases, it may be unrealistic and unreasonable to expect an agent to realize that two statements are equivalent.

The natural first reaction to this problem would be to try to develop finer identity conditions for propositions; that is, to develop a concept of proposition according to which logically equivalent statements sometimes may say different things. But if the intuitive account of propositional attitudes that we are using is right, then this reaction is a mistake. We have previously argued that the identity conditions that our theory imposes on propositions are exactly right from the point of view of the role of beliefs and desires in the rational determination of action. Hence the paradoxical consequence about logically equivalent statements is not just an unfortunate technical consequence of possible-world semantics which demands a technical solution. Rather, it is a consequence of the intuitive picture of belief and desire as determinants of action. In terms of this picture, it is not at all clear what it would mean to say that a person believed that P while disbelieving Q where P and Q are logically equivalent. There is no pattern of behavior, rational or irrational, that the hypothesis could explain. So, because I find this intuitive picture of belief and desire persuasive, I shall not respond to the problem in this way. Instead, I will take the heroic course: embrace the paradoxical consequence and try to make it palatable.

The usual way to make the consequence palatable is to admit that the functional theory of attitudes is an idealization which fits the real world only imperfectly. The ideal notions of belief and desire apply literally only to logically omniscient rational intelligences—agents whose behavior conforms strictly to a certain kind of coherent pattern. Of course no mere mortal rational agent can be expected to have a pattern of behavior which is fully coherent in every detail. The theory cannot plausibly be applied unless certain actions are set aside as actions to be explained not as consequences of some rational process, but in terms of some breakdown or limitation in the rational powers of the agent.

This admission is, I believe, correct, and it is relevant to explaining the possibility of irrational action. But it will not avoid or make palatable the paradoxical consequence for at least two reasons. First, while one might explain the *appearance* of incompatible beliefs, or the failure to believe all the equivalents of one's beliefs, in this way, one could never accept the appearance as reality. No matter how confused or irrational a person may be, one cannot consistently describe his state of mind by saying that he believes that P but fails to believe that Q where P and Q are logically equivalent, since in that case, the

proposition expressed by *P* just *is* the proposition expressed by
Q. A person can be so incoherent in his behavior that one hesi-
tates to apply the notions of belief and desire to him at all, but
his incoherence can never justify applying these notions to him
in an inconsistent way.

The second reason is that this explanation of the paradoxical
consequence seems to rule out too much as a "deviation from
the norm." One cannot treat a mathematician's failure to see
all the deductive relationships among the propositions that
interest him in this way without setting aside all of mathematical
inquiry as a deviation from rationality. But this would be
absurd. Mathematical inquiry is a paradigm of rational activity,
and a theory of rationality which excluded it from consideration
would have no plausibility.

Let us look more closely at the paradoxical consequence,
which I have expressed in a way that ignores use-mention
distinctions. It is that if a person believes that *P*, then if *P* is
logically equivalent to *Q*, he believes that *Q*. In this formulation,
the expression "that *P*" is a schema for a nominalized sentence,
which denotes some proposition. The statement "*P* is logically
equivalent to *Q*," however, is a schema for a claim about the
relation between two *sentences*. Hence the letters *P* and *Q* here
stand in for expressions that denote things that *express* the
proposition that *P*. Now once this is recognized, it should be
clear that it is not part of the allegedly paradoxical consequence
that a person must know or believe that *P* is equivalent to *Q*
whenever *P is* equivalent to *Q*. When a person believes that *P*
but fails to realize that the sentence *P* is logically equivalent
to the sentence *Q*, he may fail to realize that he believes that
Q. That is, he may fail to realize that one of the propositions
he believes is expressed by that sentence. In this case, he will
still believe that *Q*, but will not himself express it that way.

Because items of belief and doubt lack grammatical structure,
while the formulations asserted and assented to by an agent in
expressing his beliefs and doubts have such a structure, there is
an inevitable gap between propositions and their expressions.
Wherever the structure of sentences is complicated, there will
be nontrivial questions about the relation between sentences
and the propositions they express, and so there will be room
for reasonable doubt about what proposition is expressed by
a given sentence. This will happen in any account of propositions
which treats them as anything other than sentences or close
copies of sentences.

Now if mathematical truths are all necessary, there is no room for doubt about the propositions themselves. There are only two mathematical propositions, the necessarily true one and the necessarily false one, and we all know that the first is true and the second false. But the functions that determine which of the two propositions is expressed by a given mathematical statement are just the kind that are sufficiently complex to give rise to reasonable doubt about which proposition is expressed by a statement. Hence it seems reasonable to take the objects of belief and doubt in mathematics to be propositions about the relation between statements and what they say.

This suggestion is prima facie more plausible in some cases than in others. To take an easy case, if I do not recognize some complicated truth-functional compound to be a tautology, and so doubt whether what it says is true, this is obviously to be explained by doubt or error about what the sentence says. But in branches of mathematics other than logic it seems less plausible to take the objects of study to be sentences. For these cases we might take the objects of beliefs and doubts to be a common structure shared by many, but not all, of the formulations which express the necessarily true proposition. This common structure would be a kind of intermediate entity between the particular sentences of mathematics and the single, unstructured necessary proposition. In this kind of case, doubt about a mathematical statement would be doubt about whether the statements having a certain structure express the true proposition.

This suggestion for explaining mathematical ignorance and error implies that where a person fails to know some mathematical truth, there is a nonactual possible world compatible with his knowledge in which the mathematical statement says something different from what it says in this world. To develop this suggestion, one would of course have to say much more about what these nonactual possible worlds are like for particular mathematical contexts. Such a development would be a part of a theory of mathematical knowledge. I have no such account in mind, and I do not know if an account that is both plausible and consistent could be constructed. My only aim in presenting the suggestion is to show that there is at least a possibility of reconciling a possible-world theory of propositions and propositional attitudes with the rationality of mathematical inquiry.

There is a closely related problem with a parallel solution. The problem arises for those of us who have been convinced by Saul Kripke's arguments that there are necessary truths that can be known only a posteriori. That is, there are statements such that empirical evidence is required in order to know that they are true, but nevertheless they are necessarily true, and so true in all possible worlds. The best examples (although not the only ones) are identity statements containing two proper names like "Hesperus is identical to Phosphorus." It is obvious that empirical evidence is required to know that this statement is true, and it is also obvious that the relevant evidence consists of astronomical facts, and not, say, facts about meanings of words or linguistic usage. On the other hand, to see that the proposition is necessary, consider what it could mean to suppose, contrary to fact, that it were false. How could Hesperus not have been Phosphorus? It might have been that other planets— says Mars and Jupiter—were *called* Hesperus and Phosphorus, but this is not relevant. It also might have been that a different planet was seen in a certain place in the evening where Hesperus is in fact seen. But to suppose this is not to suppose that a different planet *was* Hesperus, but to suppose that it was not Hesperus which was seen in the evening. If we mean to suppose, quite literally, that Hesperus itself is distinct from Phosphorus itself, then we are just not supposing anything coherent. The planet could not have been distinct from itself.

My point is not to defend this conclusion, which is adequately done elsewhere, but to reconcile it with the thesis that propositions in the sense explained are the objects of propositional attitudes. The reason reconciliation is needed is this: consider any necessary truth which can be known only a posteriori. Since knowledge of it depends on empirical evidence which one might not have, it is possible for a person—even an ideally rational, logically omniscient person—to be ignorant of that truth. But in the possible-world account of propositional attitudes, this means that there might be a possible world compatible with the person's knowledge in which the proposition is false. But this is impossible, since the proposition is necessary, and hence true in all possible worlds. Thus it would seem that the existence of necessary but a posteriori truths is incompatible with a possible-world account of knowledge.

Let us consider what happens when a person comes to know that Hesperus is identical to Phosphorus after first being in doubt about it. If the possible-world analysis of knowledge is right, then one ought to be able to understand this change in the person's state of knowledge as the elimination of certain epistemically possible worlds. Initially, certain possible worlds are compatible with the subject's knowledge; that is, initially, they are among the worlds which the person cannot distinguish from the actual world. Then, after the discovery, these worlds are no longer compatible with the subject's knowledge. What would such possible worlds be like? If we can give a clear answer to this question, then we will have found a *contingent* proposition, which is what astronomers learned when they learned that Hesperus was identical to Phosphorus.

If we are right about the necessity of the proposition that Hesperus is identical to Phosphorus, then the possible worlds ruled out in the discovery will not be possible worlds in which Hesperus is distinct from Phosphorus, since there are none of those. Nevertheless, there are some perfectly clear and coherent possible worlds which are compatible with the initial state of knowledge but incompatible with the new one. They are worlds in which the person in question exists (since presumably he knows that he exists), and in which the proposition he would express in *that* world with the sentence "Hesperus is identical to Phosphorus" is false. That proposition will be different from the one expressed by the sentence in the actual world, since it is a contingent fact that the name "Hesperus" picks out the planet that it does pick out. Moreover, a person using the name properly might be in doubt or mistaken about this fact. In such a case, the same sentence, with the same rules of reference which determine its content, will express different propositions in different possible worlds compatible with his knowledge. It is a contingent fact that the proposition expressed is necessarily true, and it is this contingent fact which astronomers discovered.

If this is right, then the relevant object of knowledge or doubt is a proposition—a set of possible worlds—but a different one from the one that is necessarily true. There are two propositions involved, the necessary one and a contingent one. The second is a function of the rules which determine the first.

Now if the person, after finding out that Hesperus is identical to Phosphorus, were to announce his discovery by *asserting* that Hesperus is identical to Phosphorus, what would he be saying? If his assertion is really announcing his discovery, if what he is saying is what he has just come to believe, then it is the contingent proposition that he is asserting. There is generally no point in asserting the necessary proposition, although there is often a point in saying that what some statement says is necessarily true.

I will conclude my defense of the possible-world definition

of propositions by summarizing three points that I have tried
to make. First, I argued that this theory is motivated not just
by the mathematical elegance of the model-theoretic framework,
but by a familiar intuitive picture of propositional attitudes. I
suggested that this picture in part explains the heuristic power
and intuitive content of the notion of a possible world. Second,
I argued that the philosophical problems that this theory faces
are deep ones; that is, they spring from essential features of the
intuitive picture of propositional attitudes, and not from accidental and removable features of possible-world semantics. Any
account of propositional attitudes which explains them in terms
of their role in the determination of rational action, and any
account which treats the objects of these attitudes neither as
linguistic items nor as close copies of linguistic items, will be
faced with these or similar problems. Finally, I suggested that
there is at least a hope of solving the problems without giving up
the basic tenets of the theory if we recognize and exploit the
gap between propositions and the linguistic formulations which
express them. Ignorance of the truth of statements which seem
to express necessary propositions is to be explained as ignorance
of the relation between the statement and the proposition. I
have not carried out the explanation in the most difficult case
of mathematical ignorance, but I hope I have shown that such
an explanation might be possible.

COMMENTS

Lawrence Powers

Professor Stalnaker's paper exhibits his usual philosophical wit and elegance, but I cannot help but think the paper is basically wrongheaded throughout.

Before moving to my more substantial criticisms, I should like to indulge myself in railing and fulminating against a part of Stalnaker's paper that I found positively irritating. This part is a remark of his which seems to say that it does not matter if the possible-world theory is committed to the existence of nonexistent entities so long as the theory is fruitful. This remark strikes me as antiphilosophical and, if I may put it this way, offensive to right reason. Let us see how Stalnaker could have been led to such desperation.

It seems, whether rightly or wrongly, that the possible-world theory holds that there are such things as possible worlds. However, it also seems, at least at first glance, that there obviously are no such things as possible worlds. Therefore it seems that the possible-world theory is false.

I am not suggesting that the possible-world theory is not *fruitful* or *useful.* I am suggesting that it appears to be *false.* One can only wait and see whether it is useful, but one's first reaction is that any utility of the possible-world theory will be, as Russell would put it, one of the advantages of robbery over honest labor.

Indeed I know that there are many puzzles and paradoxes which the possible-world theory helps us to resolve. But this fact is irrelevant here. This fact does not show that the theory helps us to resolve the *particular* paradox before us, namely that it seems an incredible idea that there are any such things as possible worlds. In order to resolve this puzzle, we must try to spell out why it seems incredible that there should be such things and then point out those clarifications which will remove this appearance of incredibility. Perhaps Stalnaker's intuitions are so dulled that he does not find the real existence of all these possible worlds a prima facie fantastic idea. Let me try to reawaken his intuitions here.

There were in March 1972 such things as possible Democratic nominees—Muskie, Humphrey, etc. These were actual things which could become Democratic nominees. Is a possible world then an actual thing which could become or could have been a world? There are no such things. There is only one world. Nor is there something else which could turn into a world. Further, whatever exists exists in this actual world. There is no room for any other worlds.

It might be thought, though, that talk of possible worlds is not talk of actual things that could have been worlds, but rather it is talk of certain merely possible entities.

However, this suggestion runs into two problems. The first is that one of the great advantages of the possible-world theory as usually presented is that it eliminates all reference to merely possible entities. The variables of standard quantified modal logic range only over actual entities. We do not have to accept any merely possible men in order to accept standard modal logic; why then should we have to accept any merely possible entities of the species "world"?

The other difficulty is that there do not seem to be as many possible worlds as the possible-world theory seems to need.

Suppose that standing here next to me is John Doe, who has brown hair. Consider that possible world which is just like this one except that Doe's hair is green. In that world, this man John Doe has green hair. In that possible world, John Doe stands with green hair in this very room, this actual room in which we stand. This actual room is found in that world containing John Doe with green hair. In that possible world, this very planet Earth on which we stand includes this very actual room in which stands this very actual John Doe but with green hair. Similarly, this very actual solar system, this actually existing galaxy in which we actually are is found in that possible world, but there it contains a green-haired John Doe instead of a brown-haired one, although that John Doe is this very one who stands before us with brown hair. Continuing in this way, it seems that in that possible world we find always this very actual John Doe, this very room, this very galaxy, and in fact this very actual world. We do not find another John Doe, another galaxy, or—and this is the point—another world either.

I submit that the ideas that there are such things as possible worlds or that it is necessary for us to refer to nonexistent merely possible worlds—these ideas have a considerable prima facie absurdity. I submit further that these ideas are puzzling in just the ways that we would have expected a good account of modal reasoning to clear up.

I agree with Stalnaker's view that just as a scientific theory is supported by being shown to account for observations, so a philosophical theory is supported in part by being shown to account for paradoxes and puzzles. But one does not show that a theory is able to account for a given apparently adverse observation by insisting that the theory is highly supported by *other* observations. One might justifiably argue that a given apparently adverse observation will probably turn out not to be as damaging as it seems, since one's theory is otherwise so highly supported. But then one is not responding to the apparently adverse observation but only arguing that a really responsive answer will probably eventually be forthcoming. Or one may justifiably admit that a given observation really does refute one's theory and nonetheless urge that an otherwise successful theory must still be close to the truth. But if one does this, one is again not *answering* the adverse observation. One has rather admitted its force and one is now talking about expediencies.

This is just the case in Stalnaker's discussion. The various victories of the possible-world theory do lend support to that theory. But they do nothing to show that that theory is able to respond to that particular puzzle that Stalnaker is supposed to be answering, namely, that the whole idea of possible worlds (perhaps distributed in space like raisins in a pudding) seems ludicrous. To respond to this puzzle it is irrelevant to insist on the fruitfulness of the possible-world theory.

But Stalnaker's confusion about this and certain other subtle methodological points is not what I found irritating. What I found irritating was the view which Stalnaker, befuddled by the above, seemed prepared to fall into. This view is that it does not *matter* that the possible-world theory might be falsely claiming the existence of nonexistent entities so long as the theory is fruitful. On the contrary, the question whether the theory is true is the is the *only* question that philosophically matters.

Here again there is a subtle point that needs to be made clear. It might seem that theories are sometimes accepted, and properly so, because they are useful. Let us however imagine a collection of cruel sadistic nogoodniks who like to kill and torture innocent people. Accepting an empirical theory T, they find that its precepts enable them to wreak unimaginable havoc on innocent people. We know nothing else about theory T. It might be said though that we have some reason to think that

theory T is true. And we do. That fact that T is so useful to
these no-goodniks supports the theory T. But notice that we
are not inclined to accept theory T for its *utility*. It has no
utility for us. Rather the *fact* that it is so useful to those no-
goodniks suggests that, unfortunately, it is a true theory. We
sometimes accept theories because they are useful in explaining
or predicting events or in accounting for philosophical puzzles.
But this means not that we accept them for their utility and
despite their palpable untruth, but rather that we accept them
because *these* utilities are evidence for the only thing that
matters here—their truth.

If there are no such things as possible worlds and if the possible-world theory says there are, then the possible-world
theory must be rejected, however fruitful it is. Any discussion
of Stalnaker's which prepares him to deny this obvious point
must be fundamentally confused.

This is the end of my railing and ranting. I have, I suppose,
spent a lot of time attacking what amounts to a single not very
relevant sentence in Stalnaker's paper. He could easily erase this
sentence. However, some ideas seem intrinsically worth stamp-
ing out, and that sentence seems to me to be trying to express
one such idea.

It might be thought from the previous section that I have
great misgivings about possible-world theory. Actually I do not;
I just think that the phrase 'possible worlds' is misleading and
overly colorful. It might also be thought that Stalnaker does
not say anything responsive to misgivings about possible worlds.
Actually he does, as it turns out, respond directly to such
misgivings. On page 79 he suggests that instead of talking
about possible worlds, we might talk of possible states of the
world. This suggestion avoids, for instance, my "John Doe-
in this room–in this galaxy–in this world" problem.

Yet on page 84 he makes another suggestion which seems to
me to be helpful but also overdrawn. He says, "We need at
least a rudimentary notion of alternative possible situations
in order to understand such notions as belief and rational
deliberation." He continues, "If this is right, then a notion of
possible worlds is deeply involved in our ordinary ways of
regarding some of our most familiar experiences." Apparently
he thinks that when we ordinarily talk about alternative possible
situations we are talking about alternative possible *worlds*.
This seems clearly false. If I find myself in a bad situation, I

can act so as to get into a different situation. But it is impossible to get out of the actual world into some other possible world. If I know what situation I am presently in, I can act to get out of it. But if I knew which possible world (total state of affairs, past, present, and future) I was presently in, there would be nothing left to deliberate about. What we ordinarily call a "situation" is *not* a possible world.

Consider the concept of a possible lifetime fruit diet. To specify X's lifetime fruit diet is to specify all the pieces of fruit X eats in his whole lifetime. Now suppose someone offers me a choice between an apple and a banana. I am to choose between two possible (or available) pieces of fruit. Am I now choosing between possible lifetime fruit diets? Maybe the case could be conceptualized this way, but it is false that we ordinarily do conceptualize it this way. It is false that the concept of a possible lifetime fruit diet is deeply involved in our ordinary way of regarding choices between apples and bananas.

Admittedly all this cackle of mine about possible worlds is quite beside the main issues of Stalnaker's paper. I now turn to more substantial comments.

The most striking argument of Stalnaker's paper is the argument that a certain implausible theory of propositions and beliefs fits in surprisingly well with some very plausible ideas about deliberation and the role of beliefs in deliberation. I shall urge that this argument is fraudulent and actually adds no plausibility to the implausible theory about propositions and beliefs.

The implausible theory about propositions and beliefs contains the following claims. If p and q are logically equivalent propositions, they are one and the same proposition, and whoever believes p therefore believes q. Further, if p entails r, then whoever believes p believes r. Perhaps this last claim follows from the first. Whoever believes p believes $p.r$ and, if we assume that whoever believes a conjunction believes its conjuncts, then he believes r. In any case, Stalnaker's theory contains both claims.

Stalnaker says that these implausible ideas fit in well with certain plausible ideas about deliberation.

The first plausible idea about deliberation is that the notion of belief belongs to a theory intended to explain how rational creatures deliberate, and that moreover a belief is a state "which is defined or individuated by its role in determining the behavior" of the organism who has the belief. To Stalnaker this idea suggests that beliefs should be functions from possible worlds to truth values. To me, this idea suggests that, if beliefs are functions, they should be functions from desires to actions or from desires plus other beliefs to actions.

Let us try to work out a partial account of beliefs as functions to actions.

Organism X's belief that it itself is at point A will be the function which takes a desire to be at point A into an act of sitting and smiling and which takes a desire not to be at point A into an act of running away.

Its belief that it is not at point A will take a desire to not be at A into contented sitting and smiling and will take a desire to be at A into running around as if trying to get somewhere.

Now consider the diagram

$$A \longrightarrow B$$

X's belief that the arrow leads from A to B is a function which takes the belief that it (X) is at A plus a desire to be at B into the act of running along the arrow.

However, the belief that the inverse arrow leads from B to A is a quite different function. It takes X's belief that it is at B plus a desire to get to A into the act of running in the backward direction along the arrow.

Suppose now that X knows how to get from A to B but does not know how to get from B to A. Inferring X's beliefs from his actions (or propensities to act, given certain desires), we conclude that he believes that the arrow goes from A to B but does not believe (does not realize) the logically equivalent proposition that the inverse arrow leads from B to A. This example illustrates that anyone who really infers beliefs from actions will *not* say that whoever believes p believes everything that follows from p, or even everything equivalent to p. Notice further that it is wrong to say that X is not a rational agent in our example. X acts rationally in the light of his beliefs and his beliefs are furthermore consistent. His only failure is that he is not logically omniscient; he does not always know the *consequences* of his beliefs.

The above example was suggested by Jean Piaget's writings. Piaget's attempts to construct the child's conceptions of the world are real efforts to do what Stalnaker only pretends to do—namely, to envisage beliefs as functional states which help to explain actual behavior. According to Piaget, what he calls

reversibility and transitivity are difficult conceptual accomplishments. This means that knowing how to get from A to B
does *not* automatically mean knowing how to get back, and
that knowing how to get from A to B and knowing how to get
from B to C does *not* automatically mean knowing how to get
from A (through B) to C. Any serious attempt to define and/or
individuate beliefs by their roles in action would lead in the
opposite direction from Stalnaker's implausible theory of
propositions and beliefs.

But Stalnaker does not even really make any such attempt.
Rather he only asks himself what account of beliefs would fit
with a certain "simple theory" of action-determination.

This simple theory amounts to the following. One explains
why X did A, the theory says, by showing that X's beliefs *entail*
that if X does A, his desires (or presumably at least one of them)
will be satisfied.

In the first draft of Stalnaker's paper he suggested a different
simple theory: namely, that we explain why X did A by showing
that X's beliefs entail that if X's desires are satisfied, he does A.
Stalnaker has now changed the entailed proposition from "if
X's desires are satisfied, X does A" to "if X does A, X's desires
are satisfied." In either theory, though, we explain why X did A
by citing the entailments of X's beliefs.

Now Stalnaker claims that this simple theory is independently
plausible—that is, plausible independently of the assumption
that X's beliefs are deductively closed.

But is it? Suppose that X believes p, q, and r, and that p, q,
and r entail that if X is to get his desires, he must do A, or that
if X does A, he will get his desires. Suppose further that X does
not realize that his beliefs have these entailments and therefore
does not realize that doing A has any relation to his desires. Is
it then plausible to explain his doing A in terms of these entailments? Of course not.

What is "simple" about either of these simple theories is that
they both simplify matters by supposing that X's beliefs are
deductively closed.

I agree that it is a plausible procedure for someone who wants
to think about deliberation to begin by making some simplifying
assumptions or idealizations about an agent's belief structure.
Scientists quite plausibly begin with frictionless mass points
and ideal gases. But it is ludicrous to argue from the plausibility
of making idealizations to the plausibility of supposing these
idealizations to be accurate realistic truths. It is not plausible

that gases are really ideal, that this ball of cotton is a frictionless
mass point, or that the average agent's beliefs are deductively
closed.

As a final critical point, I will comment briefly on Stalnaker's
suggestion that his account can be squared with obvious facts
about mathematical knowledge. I do not see how this is going
to work. (I might note here that a certain penciled notation
on Stalnaker's first draft suggested to me that he is not unaware
of the objection I am about to raise.)
Stalnaker holds that everyone knows every necessary proposition. Therefore it implausibly follows that whoever knows all
the axioms of a branch of mathematics knows also all the esoteric
theorems. (Apparently it also follows that everyone actually
does know the axioms and theorems, but we do not need this.)
Thus mathematics really is surprisingly simple stuff! Stalnaker
suggests that perhaps the paradox can be muted by supposing
that nonetheless people sometimes know the truth of the
axiom *sentences* without knowing the truth of the theorem
sentences.
However, this is not going to work. It will not save us from
mathematical omniscience to any interesting degree. Given a
formal system, its axiom wffs, and its rules of wff-formation
and derivation, the theoremhood or nontheoremhood of given
wffs follows logically. Thus if I am logically omniscient, know
the axiom sentences and rules of derivation and sentence formation of a given mathematical system, and if I am then given a
theorem sentence, I will, as soon as I identify the sentence in
question, know that it *is* a *derivable* theorem sentence.
I may sum up so far. The possible-world theory is, I think,
true enough though misleadingly explained. Stalnaker's theory
of propositions and beliefs seems to me both implausible and
false. It cannot account for mathematical knowledge along
the lines Stalnaker suggests. Nor does reflection on deliberation
really lend any support to this theory. That this false theory
may sometimes be a fruitful and useful simplification is no
doubt true, but this fact is not enough to persuade me that
the theory is true.

Let me now beat around the surrounding bushes. There seem
to be three intriguing ideas left kicking around here. One is the
idea, suggested to me by Piaget's work, that deepening understanding of a proposition is reflected by a readier interchange

of equivalents and by a faster motion along chains of consequence. Another is Stalnaker's suggestion that propositions are not fundamentally linguistic entities and beliefs not fundamentally propensities to utter sentences. The third is that we might try to give an account of how propositions should be individuated by considering their roles in action.

The second of these three ideas is that propositions should be explained without essential reference to sentences. Notice that my simpleminded account of X getting from A to B and not back again already had this virtue. We may therefore concentrate on the first and third ideas and hope that this second one will take care of itself.

Let us envisage a theory of belief structure that will do justice to the first idea.

Imagine propositions as entities laid out in some logical space. Each proposition is a dot. Each proposition has immediate consequences and is the immediate consequence of others. Furthermore, *sets* of propositions have immediate joint consequences. For simplicity let us ignore sets. Now let each proposition be tied by an arrow to each of its immediate consequences. Therefore it is connected by a path of arrows to its farther consequences, and thus ultimately to all of its derivable consequences. Similarly it is reachable along a path of arrows from any proposition of which it is a derivable consequence. Thus the arrows fix its provable logical relations.

So far I have not mentioned belief. It seems, though, that if q is an immediate consequence of p, then believing that p should entail some readiness to believe that q. Let us postulate that if X believes p and considers p and q together, he will come to believe q. Therefore, if he believes p, he will necessarily have a tendency to come to believe p's farther and farther consequences, if he considers appropriately.

At the same time, suppose he does not believe p. Suppose q is an immediate consequence of p, and r of q. Then if he considers p, q, and r together, r will, we now postulate, become an immediate consequence for him of p. In this way, X's considerings of propositions will lead to a deeper understanding of them, which will exhibit itself in an increasing readiness to substitute logical equivalents and to move quickly along chains of logical consequence.

This picture has the weakness that I needed to postulate an unclarified relation of original immediate consequence. But it has the nice feature that at least the provable logical relations

between propositions are fixed by X's propensities to believe—
in other words, X's belief that p entails X's tendency to believe
its consequences—without having the bad feature that X's
beliefs are deductively closed.

Now let us turn to the idea that beliefs should be individuated
by their roles in action determination. The great interest of this
idea is that it seems to promise us a way to individuate propositions that would avoid on the one hand the bad idea that they
are to be individuated just like sentences, and on the other hand
the unwelcome idea that they are to be individuated à la Stalnaker by logical equivalence. As Quine has urged, the failure
to give an account of how propositions are to be individuated
is a great stumbling block to those of us who like to talk about
propositions.

Unfortunately, the intriguing idea before us seems full of
snares. In the first place, it does not seem that every proposition
is a possible belief. There are many conceivable states of affairs
in which I do not exist, but it is hard to imagine a deliberative
context in which my action is predicated on my believing that I
do not exist. Only an idealist could love a theory that makes
my existence essential to every conceivable state of affairs.

More serious difficulties are lurking here. It seems that any
action of mine could in principle be explained by saying that I
believe that certain contingencies obtain between my so acting
on the one hand and my having certain experiences of pleasure
and painlessness on the other. Suppose I am running along and,
just before slamming into a concrete wall, I skid to a halt. You
say I halted because I believed that there was a concrete wall
in front of me. But would my action have been any different if
I had *only* believed that continuing to run that way would lead
to a sudden sharp headache? It seems that the suggested way of
individuating propositions threatens to identify the proposition
that there is a wall in front of me with some conjunction of
propositions about the contingencies between actions and
experiential states. Only an idealist could be cheered by such a
way of individuating propositions.

Of course it may be objected that not all desires are desires to
have pleasures and avoid pains. I might for instance desire that
there be a wall in front of me, for instance if I am building a
house. Nor does it seem that desiring that p always amounts to
desiring pleasures and believing that p's truth will give me these
pleasures. I may desire to be buried in a certain place when I
die, but I do not thereby think that I shall be happier buried

there. I may desire that an actual living woman and not a clever robot should think me a great fellow, but I suppose that I should be as foolishly happy if I were fooled by a cleverly designed robot which looked, felt, and acted like a beautiful woman and which made noises about my being a great fellow.

Unfortunately this line of objection makes the project of defining propositions in terms of their possible roles in determining actions seem *less* and not more promising. If I can desire virtually any p, and if I can believe, however falsely, that any given action will lead to that p, the prospects for deducing my beliefs from my actions seems dim indeed.

Alternatively, if basic desires are simple desires for pleasure and painlessness, then the project of defining propositions in terms of their roles in action seems nothing less than a project of describing a constitution of the external world out of experiential contingencies. That Stalnaker's theory of propositions does not face these extraordinarily large difficulties is, I think, simply an indication of the fact that he is not seriously attempting to define and individuate beliefs in the way he suggests. He is just whistling about it.

A FURTHER REMARK

One may wish to object to my A-to-B example along the following lines. X believes that he can move from A to B by running along the arrow but does not believe that he can move from B to A by running backward along it. These propositions are not equivalent. There might be a guard on the arrow who allows only one-way traffic, so that X can get from A to B along the arrow, but cannot get back the same way. However, this still does not explain why X does not at least try going back along the arrow.

It is just this type of difficulty with really working out my example which leads me to think that only action-contingency statements can be plausibly derived from propensities to act. If my example is not an example of failing to realize that the inverse arrow goes from B to A, what on earth would be? Further, note that this kind of objection works only against reversibility problems and does not help against transitivity.

REMARKS ON REFERENCE AND ACTION

Charles Landesman

In recent discussions of reference, it has become customary to admit that it is not words in themselves that refer to things in the world, but that it is persons who refer to things by using words in their linguistic actions. It is conceded that words acquire their referential connections to the world as a result of what people do with them. It follows that the claim that a particular word refers to particular thing is just an abbreviated way of saying that persons in the speech community use that word to refer to that thing. Referring as an action, as something that people do, is prior in the order of explanation to reference as a semantic relation between a word and an object.

It is one thing to make an admission like this; it is another thing to take it seriously, to follow it up, and to draw out its consequences. In speaking about language, philosophers often take it for granted that words are merely one kind of thing among other kinds in the world, that, like other things in the world, words have various relations to objects, and that these relations can be investigated, formulated, and systematized. Occasionally in the preface to such an investigation, it is admitted that discourse does exist in human action and for the sake of attaining human ends, and that this mode of existence is the explanatory basis of the relations which words come to have to objects. Carnap, for example, has noted that there is an empirical inquiry, which he calls pragmatics, whose subject is actual living discourse; semantics is merely an abstraction from pragmatics. He writes: "If we wish to investigate language as a human activity, we must take into consideration all those factors connected with speaking activities. But the sentences and the signs (e.g., words) occurring in them are sometimes involved in another relation. A sign or expression may concern or designate something, or, rather, he who uses the expression may intend to refer to something by it."[1] Carnap here recognizes that the relation of

---

1. Rudolf Carnap, "Foundations of Logic and Mathematics," *International Encyclopedia of Unified Science* (Chicago: University of Chicago Press, 1955), 1: 145–46.

designation that words bear to things is in some way constituted by the activities of those who use words. I do not think, however, that he takes any of this very seriously; certain puzzles arise as a result of his not really thinking through how semantic relations are constituted by linguistic action. An example of a puzzle is this: in pragmatics, the assertion that a certain word in English, say "five," refers to a certain number is an empirical claim to be tested by observing the behavior of speakers of English. In semantics, however, the parallel claim that "five" designates 5 turns out to be analytic.[2] It is natural to wonder how an empirical and contingent connection turns into an analytic connection through an act of abstraction. Perhaps an explanation can be found. But it seems to be that the allusion to pragmatics is a form of conventional piety, whereas it is semantics that constitutes the living part of the faith.

Even those whose primary interest is in pragmatics or in the theory of speech acts occasionally commit lapses which make one wonder. For example, J. L. Austin in his lectures *How to Do Things with Words* attempts to distinguish between a locutionary act "which is roughly equivalent to uttering a certain sentence with a certain sense and reference" and the illocutionary act which is the speech act per se.[3] He seems to suggest that the illocutionary act presupposes the locutionary act, that the illocutionary act just is the locutionary act with something special added to it, the illocutionary force. The referential power of words is taken to be logically prior to their power to occur in full-fledged speech acts. If that is so, then their occurrence in speech acts cannot be used to explicate their referential power.

If we wish to take seriously the claim that words acquire their referential connections to objects in the world through human action, through persons doing things with words, then there is a broad and general view of language which entitles us to take it seriously. I shall first provide a brief and rough sketch of this view without any attempt at justification except its intrinsic plausibility. Then I shall devote the remainder of this paper to extracting some of its implications for the topic of referring.

In general, what gives life to language are the actions in which words are used by speakers to attain their ends and purposes. The categories of meaning and reference come to apply to sounds

2. Rudolf Carnap, "Empiricism, Semantics, and Ontology," in his *Meaning and Necessity*, (Chicago: University of Chicago Press, 1956), p. 217.

3. J. L. Austin, *How to Do Things with Words* (Oxford: Oxford University Press, 1962), p. 108.

as a result of what the agents who produce them want to do
with them. Syntactic structures as well acquire their functions
in the context of human action. That certain sounds are meaningful units of discourse and that certain patterned sequences of
sounds exemplify grammatical structures are matters of convention. The regularities of speech are conventional, not natural,
and conventions are but human artifacts constituted by human
purposive activity; conventions are the products of action; they
are not laws of nature. The reality of language lies in linguistic
action, that is, in words being used by speakers to say certain
things for certain purposes. The forms of language abstracted
from linguistic actions are just that, abstractions, not the concrete reality of language itself. It is true, of course, that knowledge of these abstractions is essential to the ability to speak and
to interpret the discourse of others. The reason why this knowledge is essential is that these forms exist in discourse itself.

The speech community as a whole is in the position of Humpty
Dumpty in that famous passage from *Through the Looking
Glass.* " 'When I use a word,' Humpty Dumpty said, in a rather
scornful tone, 'it means just what I choose it to mean—neither
more nor less.' 'The question is,' said Alice, 'whether you *can*
make words mean so many different things.' 'The question is,'
said Humpty Dumpty, 'which is to be master—that's all.' "[4]
Words mean what members of the speech community make
them mean, not necessarily through deliberate choice, but
through collective action. The community is the master; it
creates the conventions of language. The individual as well can
become the master of his own linguistic conventions. This is
not as easy, however, as Humpty Dumpty implies, because, in
creating conventions that diverge from the community's, he
has to overcome fixed habits of his own. And also, as when
Humpty Dumpty used the word "glory" to mean "there's a
nice knock-down argument for you," he will have difficulty
making himself understood.

These general considerations about language suggest that a
difference that makes no difference from the perspective of
what people do and think is not a difference with respect to
what they mean or with respect to the objects meant or referred
to. In discussions of reference it is not unusual to find that the
writer is trying to make a distinction between a word's actually
referring to or naming something and its purporting to or

4. Lewis Carroll, *Through the Looking Glass* (New York: Random
House, 1946), p. 94.

attempting to refer.[5] The concept of reference has often been used so that someone who is trying to refer to something can succeed in what he is trying to do only if certain extralinguistic conditions are satisfied. The condition that is most often mentioned is that the object referred to must exist, where to say that it exists means that it does or has or will exist. Thus, someone who utters the sentence "Napoleon was a great general" in order to make the statement that Napoleon was a great general has used the word "Napoleon" to refer to something, whereas someone who utters the sentence "Pegasus was a winged horse" fails to refer to anything because there exists no such thing with the name "Pegasus." Although "Pegasus" is syntactically similar to a referring expression like "Napoleon," an essential condition, in this view, for its being a referring expression is missing. In this way of looking at the matter, the word "refer" is understood as an achievement verb. One may try to refer to something, but, because the existence condition is not satisfied, one fails. One may believe that he has been referring to a certain object for a long period of time, and suddenly find out that because there is no such object he was not actually referring at all.

From the perspective of the agent who is using words there need not be any difference between referring and merely trying to refer. Both in the case in which the existence condition is satisfied and in the case in which it is not, he may use a proper name or other singular term thinking that there exists something named by that term. The difference has nothing to do with what the agent is conscious of; it is not a difference in what he means and thinks, but rather in whether or not something that he means in fact exists. It is puzzling, however, to try to understand how the question whether a certain object exists has anything to do with which object he means. For unless he knows which one he means, it is difficult to understand how he might even begin to inquire whether what he means actually exists. I do not wish to deny that "refer" is an achievement verb; various sorts of mistakes are possible in our use of singular terms, and these lead to various sorts of failures. But I do not think that the consummation of an act of referring depends upon the existence of the item referred to. I do not think an existence condition is implied by the concept of referring that we do have, nor can I think of any good reason for replacing our present

5. For example, see W. V. Quine, *Methods of Logic* (New York: Holt, Rinehart and Winston, 1964), p. 197.

concept with one that does imply an existence condition. When we listen to someone who is speaking of some object, who is using words to mention that object and to say something about it, then there is some action he is performing which we can know he is performing quite independently of whether we know that some existence condition has been satisfied. That action is referring. It is necessary to distinguish those concepts that are required in order to interpret human discourse as discourse from those that designate particular de facto relations that bits of discourse bear to bits of the real world.

Occasionally one finds in discussions of reference that conditions that are very often satisfied when referring takes place are mistaken for conditions that are essential to reference as such. For example, John Searle claims that in singular reference, "the speaker picks out or identifies some particular object which he then goes on to say something about, or to ask something about, etc."[6] He describes the act of referring as having as its distinctive function picking out or identifying some object. Clearly what he has in mind is a type of context in which a speaker says something about something to someone else. He assumes that this type of context is characteristic of all cases of reference.[7] In a conversation there is a point at which the hearer does not yet know which object the speaker is going to talk about. If communication is to be successful, the speaker must convey to the hearer which object it is. In this view, referring is that speech act by means of which the speaker picks out or identifies the object for the hearer.

This approach ignores one very important circumstance which any adequate theory must take account of. This is the fact that we not only say things to others but we often say things to ourselves; not only do we say things out loud, but we also say them under our breath. There are mental as well as overt acts of assertion. Thinking as well as speaking is often involved. Following an old usage, I shall call the act of asserting something to oneself a judgment. To take an example, I see a gray rock and I make the judgment that the rock is gray. In my judgment I refer to the rock and I ascribe a certain color to it. Many of our judgments are made in words, or, at least, in verbal imagery. But judgments can also be formulated using nonverbal materials. It can be sufficient for a judgment that I form a visual image

6. John Searle, *Speech Acts* (Cambridge University Press, 1969), p. 81.
7. Ibid., p. 80.

of the gray rock in an assertive frame of mind. A judgment is a
symbolic mental act; whether or not it is also a linguistic act
depends upon the particular symbolic materials used.

Descriptions of linguistic actions which apply to overt speech
acts do not necessarily apply to covert acts such as judgments.
In particular, I do not think that the notions of identifying or
picking something out are applicable. With judgments there are
no other persons for whom the reference identifies or picks out
an object. And I do not think that it is particularly enlightening
to say that in an interior monologue the self can be understood
as performing the dual functions of speaker and hearer. Private
ruminations are not exactly like conversations with others. When
I say something to myself, there is no problem of not knowing
which object I intend to describe to myself as gray. If I did not
know which it was then I could not even pick it out. But since
I do know which it is, I do not have to pick it out or identify
it to myself. (There are special cases in which one remembers
the predicate but forgets the subject. Something is gray but
which object is it? In these cases, there is something going on
analogous to picking out or identifying. But although it is
analogous, it is not just the same, since it is a form of remembering.) In judgment, the act of referring is simply the way one
is conscious of the object the judgment is about. When I judge
that the rock is gray, I do not merely know which thing it is
to which I am ascribing the color gray, but I am also exercising
that knowledge. Referring to the object as "the rock" is the
form that this exercise of knowledge takes. What is true of the
judgment also applies to the corresponding overt linguistic action.
When I say out loud that the rock is gray, I am, at the very least,
exercising my knowledge of which object is gray. I may also
be doing something else, such as identifying that object for
someone else. The transition from covert symbolical acts to
overt speech may be accompanied by and may even be motivated
by the addition of new functions for the linguistic act one is
performing. But if one wants a theory of the essential conditions
of linguistic actions, he will have to bring in conditions that
hold for covert as well as overt episodes, and he will have to
put aside conditions that are characteristic mainly of overt
episodes.

Earlier I argued that a common error in discussions of reference is stipulating that the existence of the object referred to is
necessary for there to be a reference to that object in the first

place. There is a related error in thinking that its existence is also a necessary condition for the truth of the statement made. In some views, existence is a necessary condition for the statement to be either true or false, or even for there to be a statement at all. In others, existence is a necessary condition for truth merely; if the object fails to exist, the statement turns out to be false. Right now, I shall consider only what is common to both these types of view.

These errors are clearly related. Each serves to justify the other. First consider how the existence condition for reference serves to justify an existence condition for truth. Suppose the object allegedly referred to fails to exist. Then, if reference presupposes existence, one has not referred to anything. Therefore, there is nothing about which one has said something true. Therefore, one has not succeeded in making a true statement. So it seems that in order to make a true statement there must exist an object referred to. Now consider how an existence condition for truth leads to one for reference. Again we suppose that the object allegedly referred to fails to exist. If truth presupposes existence, then one has not made a true statement. But what stands in the way of truth here? If one has actually succeeded in referring to an object, what stands in the way of simply predicating something true of it? The only thing that can prevent a true statement from being made is that one has not actually referred to anything. Since both conditions stand together, they also fall together. And so the considerations I have presented against the existence condition for reference also apply to the existence condition for truth.

Now the claim that truth presupposes existence yields some strange and counterintuitive results. Since the Greek god Zeus never really existed, the obvious truth that Zeus was a Greek god turns out to be either an obvious falsehood or something that is neither true nor false. And the obvious truth that Zeus never existed is said not to be a statement about Zeus. But if no object has been said not to exist, then I fear that nothing has been said. Only if one can make some sense of the dogma that existence is not a property which things may have or lack can our intuitions be overridden.

These difficulties with the existence condition have not gone unnoticed, and one can detect certain back-door attempts to avoid meeting them head on. Thus after formulating an existence condition for reference which he calls the "axiom of existence," Searles argues that references to fictions do not count against

the axiom. "One can refer to them as fictional characters precisely because they exist in fiction. . . . Sherlock Holmes does
not exist at all, which is not to deny that he exists-in-fiction."[8]
This sounds like an attempt to have your cake and also to eat
it. If Sherlock Holmes does not exist at all, one would think
that the axiom of existence would apply to the alleged statement that Sherlock Holmes was a great detective and that no
reference to a particular detective was actually made. And if he
does not exist at all, in what sense, then, does he exist-in-fiction?
If this is just another way of saying that he is a fictional character, then Searle has in effect conceded my point, and his so-
called axiom of existence should really be entitled the axiom
of subsistence.

Someone who insists on the existence condition for reference
has, I think, even a further difficulty. Overt referential action
can also be performed in the course of making a judgment.
Anything that can be referred to can be thought of, and anything that can be thought of can be referred to. Thus an existence
condition for verbal reference requires an existence condition
for thought. Not only can I not mention aloud in words something that does not exist, but I cannot even think about it. And
this seems to be implausible. Suppose one is thinking about
something, say about Zeus, believing him to exist. This accompanying belief is false. But it does not follow, it seems to me,
that one was mistaken in what it was that one thought he was
thinking about. If one is questioned whether he was really
thinking of Zeus, he could mention all sorts of properties Zeus
possesses, and in this way identify the object of thought as
Zeus. I see no other way to individuate thoughts, to distinguish
the thought of Zeus from the thought of Pegasus, except by
reference to the fact that each is a thought of a different object.

Advocates of the existence condition may suggest some reductionist account as a way of saving the day. According to one
version, in the case of statements apparently about fictional
or mythological entities, what one is really talking about is not
a nonexistent entity but the actual speech and beliefs of real
people. To say, for example, that Zeus was a Greek god is to
say something about the beliefs or the statements of the ancient
Greeks. Now there is a major reason against relying upon reductionist accounts which I shall get to later. A less important
reason is that the whole problem reappears in trying to make
sense of the reductionist account. For which statements and

8. Ibid., pp. 78–79.

which beliefs are we talking about when we say that Zeus was a Greek god? It must be those statements and those beliefs of the ancient Greeks which are 'about' Zeus.

A potential source of scepticism about my argument so far may be a concern for the fate of our standard logical systems. If a statement of the form "x refers to y" does not entail that there exists something that x refers to, one begins to wonder whether we are not in for some sort of nonstandard logic. What, for example, happens to the rule of existential generalization? Is some alternative rule required?

Recently worries of this sort have invaded the ostensibly unrelated domain of aesthetics. In his *The Languages of Art*, Nelson Goodman argues that pictorial representation is a form of referring or denoting. A picture of the Duke of Wellington, for example, actually refers to or denotes the Duke of Wellington. Pictures function like names and descriptions. But what about a picture of Pickwick or a picture of a unicorn? There does not exist anything for these pictures to refer to. Goodman's way of dealing with the problem is to claim that a statement of the form "x is a picture of y" is ambiguous.[9] Either it means that x refers to y and hence that y exists, or it is simply a way of describing the sort of picture x is. Thus to say that something is a picture of a unicorn is not to say that it refers to unicorns, since there are no unicorns to refer to; it is simply to say that it is a unicorn-picture.

Suppose a person is walking up and down a gallery identifying the pictures hanging on the wall. "That's a picture of the Duke of Wellington, there's one of Pickwick, that is a picture of Cromwell, and there is a unicorn," he says, in each case being fully aware of what does and what does not exist. It seems to me that it is quite implausible to say that his use of the phrase "picture of" changes its meaning, depending on the accompanying belief about existence, as he moves from one picture to the next. The motive for this implausible claim is to protect existential generalization. If we were to say that something is a picture of Pickwick, leaving "Pickwick" subject to quantification, then, it is assumed, we would be saying something false.

This assumption is, however, quite problematic. Following Lejewski,[10] I shall call the quantifier in question the particular

9. Nelson Goodman, *The Languages of Art* (Indianapolis: Bobbs-Merrill, 1969), p. 22.
10. Czeslaw Lejewski, "Logic and Existence," *British Journal for the Philosophy of Science* (1955).

quantifier for reasons that will be apparent in a moment. Now this assumption involves the broader claim that in the standard logic it is necessary to give an existential interpretation to the particular quantifier. Thus, Quine writes: "The existential quantifier, in the objectual sense, is given precisely the existential interpretation and no other: there are things which are thus and so."[11] However, one has failed to fix the existential interpretation by explaining it merely as meaning that there are things which are thus and so. The reason is that there is a use of the phrase "there is" which is ontologically neutral or noncommittal. It is clearly exemplified in fictional discourse. It also occurs in discourse in which the existence of a certain object is to be left an open question. For example, although I might be willing to affirm the truth of the statement that there is a number between two and four, I might be unwilling to concede that numbers really exist. To the question "Do numbers exist?" I may be unprepared to give an answer, although I am willing to affirm countless arithmetical truths about numbers. Again, the use of the noncommittal interpretation is exemplified in aesthetic discourse. In looking at a picture, I may see a certain object, say a fat man dressed in a green suit. I may describe this person in some detail. I am not thereby describing the painting, for the painting is not a man although it is of a man. I am talking of the represented object, or, if you like, the object of my vision. I may be ignorant of whether that man ever really existed. I may wish to hold the question of his existence in abeyance. But that there is a subject of discourse as well as an object of vision about which I can say a great deal just by looking at the painting is beyond doubt. The phrase "there is" used in this ontologically neutral way I shall call simply the noncommittal interpretation of the quantifier. In this interpretation, to say that there is a such and such does not entail that there exists a such and such; moreover, the statement that everything exists turns out to be false.

I wish to make two points with regard to the noncommittal interpretation. In the first place, it is not simply one interpretation among others, but has, I think, a privileged place in logic. This has been obscured by the fact that recent discussions of ontological commitment have made the existential interpretation of the particular quantifier seem to be its natural or privileged use. But there is a more fundamental role for logic than

11. W. V. Quine, *Ontological Relativity and Other Essays* (New York: Columbia University Press, 1969), p. 106.

clarifying ontological commitments. Logic is our most general
theory of ratiocination. It is an instrument for the critical
analysis of inferences that occur outside of ontology as well
as within it. In this role, it is important to be able to formulate
inferences in a way which is metaphysically neutral. We ought,
for example, to be able to do arithmetic without having to make
a prior decision on the nominalism-realism issue. In a context
innocent of metaphysical purpose we might wish to investigate
whether the following argument is valid: Any integer greater
than 4 and less than 6 is prime; 5 is an integer greater than 4
and less than 6; therefore 5 is prime; therefore there is a prime
number, namely five. We should agree that this inference is
valid, and yet when we turn to ontology we may very well
wonder whether numbers really exist. While various forms of
discourse raise problems for metaphysics, they do not settle
them. Therefore we need a quantifier which does not create an
ontological commitment. In its function as an instrument of
ratiocination, logic must be applicable to forms of discourse
even prior to a metaphysically acceptable interpretation of that
discourse. The noncommittal interpretation can do that job. As
a further benefit, it allows quantification over predicate and
propositional variables while leaving the existence of attributes
and propositions an open question.

In the second place, the noncommittal interpretation of the
particular quantifier does not lead to any changes in the usual
rules for logic. There are nonstandard systems which keep the
existential interpretation but allow the use of singular terms
that fail to refer to existents. Changes in the rules are usually
required. In one such system existential generalization becomes
Fa, therefore $(Ex)(x = a) \supset (Ex)Fx$. This rule is unnecessarily
restrictive. One would like to infer from the fact that Pegasus
was a winged horse that something was a winged horse, without
having to certify the prior existence of winged horses. Alternative logics become unnecessary under the noncommittal interpretation. Moreover, the existential interpretation of the particular quantifier becomes superfluous. If we wish to engage in
discourse in order to clarify our ontological commitments, we
merely introduce the predicate "exists," retaining the quantifier
in its noncommittal form. And this is a philosophical advantage.
Given the primary purpose of logic as the theoretical basis for
the analysis of reasoning about any subject matter whatever,
there is no reason to think that existence is a logically privileged
concept. If we want logic to be topic-neutral and to be able to

capture inferences about nonexistent things, then existence
should not be built into the meaning of the quantifier.

One might wonder how the noncommittal interpretation of
the quantifier might affect the usual way of providing semantic
interpretations of logical formulas. Roughly, an interpretation
of a formula is an assignment of a denotation or reference to
each of the nonlogical constants and to the free variables of the
formula, and a truth value to the sentence letters. Obviously, if
a certain entity is assigned to a certain sign in a formula, then
something is assigned to that sign. If we employ the noncommittal interpretation of the particular quantifier when it occurs
in the semantic metalanguage, then the statement that a certain
entity has been assigned to a certain sign does not commit us
to the existence of the entity so assigned. Thus nothing in the
standard accounts need be changed. And there is a genuine gain
in the freedom we now have to draw interpretations from
universes of discourse without having to worry about the reality
of entities within these universes.

I should like to discuss one further related point on the topic
of reference. If we consider an affirmative statement formulated
in a sentence of subject-predicate form such as "The rock is
gray," I do not see that it is reasonable to say, as is so often
said, that whereas the subject term "the rock" is used to refer
to a certain particular, the predicate term "gray" does not refer
at all. While it is often conceded that the predicate term has an
extension which consists of the class of objects of which the
term is true, it is just as often denied, usually in the interests of
an ontology suspicious of such abstractions as attributes, that
the predicate refers to any property or feature of the object to
which the subject term refers. I want to argue, on the contrary,
that "gray" does refer to a certain color. I am willing to claim
even further that the sentence as a whole is used to refer to that
state of affairs which, should it exist, would make the corresponding statement true. I shall, however, confine my remarks
to the first claim.

There is a standard argument against the view that predicates
can have a referential function.[12] It goes like this. If "gray"
refers to the color gray, then it refers to the same thing as "the
color gray." But if, according to the rule that co-referential
terms may be substituted for one another *salva veritate*, we
replace "gray" by "the color gray" in "The rock is gray," what

12. Searle, *Speech Acts*, pp. 102, 103.

we end up with is a sentence which by one interpretation is just false, and by another is unintelligible. Substitutivity is a requirement of referential position, and, so the argument goes, predicates fail to pass the test. Therefore, predicates are not referring expressions. This is not, I think, a very good argument. In the example under discussion, a term of one grammatical category, a noun phrase, was substituted for a term of an entirely distinct grammatical category, an adjective. It is not surprising that the sentence with which we ended up is grammatically problematic. If we allow the terms we substitute to be drawn from different categories from those substituted for, we could prove that singular terms do not refer. The rule of substitutivity requires at least that the substitute be in the appropriate category. In fact what the argument does prove is that the terms do not belong to the same category. Bergmann has pointed out[13] that if we insist upon drawing terms from different categories we must make suitable grammatical adjustments. Thus if in "The rock is gray" we replace "is" by "exemplifies," then it is all right to replace "gray" by "the color gray."

There is another argument that I would like to mention against the referential function of predicates. It assumes that in the use of a subject-predicate sentence to make a statement, the subject term has a function quite distinct from the predicate term. To use Strawson's language, subjects and predicates *introduce* entities into discourse in different ways.[14] Thus in "The rock is gray," "the rock" is used to introduce a particular by referring to it, whereas "gray" is used to introduce a quality by predicating it of or ascribing it to the rock. There are, according to this argument, two functions which need to be kept distinct from one another.

Without denying that some such functional distinction exists, I want to make two remarks about it. In the first place, it is, in a sense, a linguistic accident; it is not fundamental in the sense of being inevitable or inescapable. For example, instead of using predicates to ascribe a quality to a subject, we could have a language in which predicates are replaced by abstract singular terms. "The rock exemplifies grayness" would then replace "The rock is gray." In that case, the quality "gray" would not be introduced in a manner different from the way the particular is introduced. Instead of conveying the information that the

13. Gustav Bergmann, *Meaning and Existence* (Madison: University of Wisconsin Press, 1960), p. 220.
14. P. F. Strawson, *Individuals* (London: Methuen, 1959), p. 146.

rock is gray by using a predicate to ascribe grayness to the rock, one could convey the same information by using "grayness" to refer to the color which the rock exemplifies.

In the second place, that a term has a certain function does not exclude it from simultaneously having another. In fact, one function may very well presuppose a second. In the case of the singular term "the rock," the reason this phrase is selected as the one used to refer to a certain particular is that it alludes to a species of mineral as the species to which the particular belongs. One way of referring to a thing is referring to it as something or other, and this requires or presupposes an allusion to a classification. Similarly, in order to ascribe a color to the rock, we must tell which color it is, and the predicate term "gray" does just that. The function of ascription presupposes the function of reference. If the predicate did not refer to or indicate a certain color, then how could it be used to ascribe just that color to the rock? There are things that subjects and predicates both do in the course of being used to make a statement or to form a judgment: they both function to point, so to speak, to entities which the statement or judgment brings together in a certain way.

The referring function is common to a variety of functions that a predicate may be used to perform. Consider the following three sentences:

1. The rock is gray.
2. The rock is not gray.
3. Is the rock gray?

It is only in (1) that "gray" is used to ascribe a color to an object. In (2) it is used to deny that color of an object, and in (3) it is used to interrogate an object with respect to that color. In order to understand each of these sentences, it is necessary to know which is the color in question. In all three, it is "gray" that is used to tell which it is.

A nominalist may be inclined to complain that I have been populating the universe with an undesirable plurality of abstract entities. But the charge that I am encouraging a population explosion really amounts to a misunderstanding. For if, in the statement that there is a quality to which "gray" refers, the quantifier is interpreted noncommittally, then the problem of the existence and status of the abstraction is left an open question. And this is as it should be, for we can tell what we mean without having a theory of the way the world is.

COMMENTS

Jay F. Rosenberg

This is a grand, old-fashioned, gauntlet-flinging paper Professor Landesman has produced for us, chock-full of charming heresies. Among the theses nailed to the church door are these six:

1. That the existence of the object referred to is not a necessary condition of successful reference,
2. That, consequently, it is not necessary that the object of reference exist in order that a statement be made or that the statement made be true,
3. That the distinctive function of an act of referring is not that of picking out or identifying an object,
4. That quantification in its *primary* use is ontologically noncommittal, whether over individual variables or over predicate and propositional variables,
5. That, consequently, as concerns logic, existence is, or can be introduced as, a real predicate, and
6. That logical predicates are referring expressions.

And from what springs this new revelation? Well, it is opened unto us, we're told, once we disabuse ourselves of some misconceptions about language. Specifically, we must stop setting language up as a graven image, stop viewing words as "merely one kind of thing among other kinds in the world." For what it really *is* is Humpty Dumpty writ large.

> What gives life to language are the actions in which words are used by speakers to attain their ends and purposes. . . . The regularities of speech are conventional, not natural, . . . conventions are the products of action; they are not laws of nature. The reality of language lies in linguistic action. . . . The speech community as a whole is in the position of Humpty Dumpty in that famous passage from *Through the Looking Glass* (pp. 106–107).

Well, one would hope not *exactly* the same position, for it was shortly after the discourse with Alice that Humpty Dumpty took his notorious *fall*, wasn't it? And, anyway, the *Looking Glass* episode is marked as dubious and apocryphal in the authorized biography of Mr. Dumpty.[1]

1. Clifford Irving, *Humpty Dumpty: The Egg Behind the Myth* (New York: McGraw-Hill, forthcoming).

119

Not, of course, that anyone would *disagree* with Professor
Landesman's general remarks about language. For what's the
alternative? Adam receiving a crash Berlitz course in Indo-
European from God in Eden on the sixth day? (Although it may
be the case that there are inherent genetic constraints on the
forms of humanly possible languages.) But surely such striking
victories over contemporary Anglo-American orthodoxy cannot
be won so handily from such an uncontroversial basis. Let's
look into the matter.

I am golfing, and, on the par 3 fifteenth, I hit a lovely 2-iron
shot which clears the water, lands on the green, rolls up to the
pin, and stops. But it does not drop, for the greenskeeper has
this day perversely neglected to supply the *hole.* The flag is
simply jammed into the grass.

Now Landesman argues for his first heresy—that the existence
of the object referred to is not a necessary condition of successful reference—on the ground that "a difference that makes no
difference from the perspective of what people do and think is
not a difference with respect to . . . the objects meant or referred
to." Such is the case with the putative distinction between
successfully referring and merely trying to refer but failing for
want of an extant object to refer *to.*

> From the perspective of the agent who is using words there
> need not be any difference between referring and merely
> trying to refer. Both in the case in which the existence con-
> dition is satisfied and in the case in which it is not, he may
> use a proper name or other singular term thinking that there
> exists something named by that term. The difference has
> nothing to do with what the agent is conscious of; it is not a
> difference in what he means and thinks, but rather in whether
> or not something that he means in fact exists (p. 108).

But from my perspective on the fifteenth tee, there need not
be any difference between making a hole-in-one and merely
trying to make one. Both in the case in which there is a hole
in the fifteenth green and in the case in which there is not, I
address and strike a golf ball, believing it to be directed toward
a hole. That difference has nothing to do with what I am conscious of. Yet I cannot make a hole-in-one without a hole. The
rules of golf are as human an artifact as the conventions of
language, yet the *successful consummation of a golf objective*
depends upon the behavior of greenskeepers (and many other
factors as well—the wind direction and velocity, for example)

as much as on the beliefs, intentions, and activities of the golfer. And this is true of many human actions. I cannot poison the people in the house by operating the pump which supplies their drinking water unless the water is, in fact, poisoned, and unless they cooperate at least to the extent of drinking the poisoned water. The successful consummation of many human actions—conventional and nonconventional—depends essentially upon the satisfaction of conditions external to the beliefs, intentions, and behaviors of the agent. We need an argument to show that referring is not such an action and the existence of the object such an external condition.

Now Landesman writes of an agent engaged in putative reference that

> it is puzzling . . . to try to understand how the question whether a certain object exists has anything to do with which object he means. For unless he knows which one he means, it is difficult to understand how he might even begin to inquire whether what he means actually exists (p. 108).

This sounds compelling. Yet there is something odd about the conduct of his case here. For the defender of referential orthodoxy will surely insist that in the problematic cases *there isn't any* "object he means" and, hence, Landesman, in using the phrases "which one he means" and "what he means" has *himself* failed to refer. It is question-begging, in other words, to put the orthodox position, as Landesman does, as laying down the condition that "the object referred to must exist." *That* can't be the orthodox existence condition. For whatever the orthodox existence condition is, the failure to meet it is supposed to guarantee that no *referring* has occurred, and, hence, that there isn't any *object referred to*. The orthodox existence condition does not, as Landesman would have it, presuppose that some object *is* referred to and then lay down requirements about *it*, for example that it exist.

What the orthodox existence condition does talk about, of course, is not the object referred to but the putatively referring *expression*—the proper name or description used by the speaker. It is the requirement that there exist an object answering to that name or satisfying that description. If there exists no such object, in the orthodox account, then no referring has occurred and no object has been referred to.

Now I accept the intent of Landesman's first heresy, and with it that of his second—that satisfaction of the existence condition

is not a necessary condition of a statement's being made or of
the statement which is made being true. But *my* argument has
nothing to do with Humpty Dumpty. It is the fine old Scholastic
tract: *ab esse, ad posse*. We *do* refer to lots of things that don't
exist, and from this it follows that we *can*. But there are cases
and cases here. Landesman concentrates on fiction, and that
is one sort of case. But there is another sort, made famous by
Donnellan, where the orthodox existence condition fails and
yet we succeed in referring to something which, unlike a fictional entity, *does* exist. Thus, I may use in discussion the
expression 'an important unpublished manuscript of Saul
Kripke's' and, although nothing exists which satisfies this
description, for Saul Kripke never writes anything down, I may
succeed in referring to what we all know does exist, namely
an important untranscribed lecture tape of Saul Kripke's. And
there is the third sort of case—which, after all, *started* all this
existence business—where I use a noun phrase built up quite
arbitrarily, say, 'the tallest building in my living room', and,
noting that there are no buildings in my living room, it is here
the case that I actually *do* fail to refer to anything. And while
I surely do say something when I say that the tallest building in
my living room is made entirely of polished Carrara marble,
unlike my saying that Pegasus had wings or that the beautiful
sorceress who ruled the Quadlings of Oz rode in a swan-driven
chariot, it is difficult to get my "tallest building" remark into
the true-false line of work.

   Actually, I suspect that the third sort of case didn't occur to
Landesman at all (although both Meinong's famous "golden
mountain" and Russell's infamous "present king of France"
were of *that* sort). For he has something *like* an existence condition implicitly going for him, I think. Although Pegasus does
not *exist*, since the particular quantifier is ontologically noncommittal (that's the fourth heresy), *there is* such a thing as
Pegasus. That is, '$(Ex)(x = $ Pegasus)' is true, and presumably
necessarily so, since it follows from 'Pegasus = Pegasus' by the
usual rules of logic. So it looks like there is a 'there is' condition
for successful reference à la Landesman.

   By the way, is the fourth heresy true? Well, Landesman has
a nice sort of argument for it. The argument has nothing in
particular to do with the artifactuality of language, however,
but concerns the fundamental role, job, or function of logic as

   our most general theory of ratiocination. It is an instrument
   for the critical analysis of inferences that occur outside of

ontology as well as within it. In this role, it is important to be able to formulate inferences in a way which is metaphysically neutral (p. 115).

Now this is pretty good, so let's accept the fourth heresy, but with a few cautionary glosses. For one thing, the *negation* of the particular quantifier seems *always* to carry a bit of ontological clout. While it seems perfectly all right to say that there are many things which don't exist—we can give examples: Pegasus, Pickwick, Sherlock Holmes—it isn't similarly all right to say of some things that exist that there aren't any such things. That so-and-so does not exist, in other words, doesn't entail the falsity of 'there is such a thing as so-and-so', but that there *isn't* such a thing as so-and-so *does* entail the falsity of 'so-and-so exists'. Even a noncommittal quantifier can't stay noncommittal when negation rolls around. And this needs to be explained.

Second, the ontologically noncommittal interpretation of the particular quantifier may be logically primary in an important sense, but this must not obscure the fact that there are quite a few common *committal uses* of the quantifier. That was one.

And, now, third, one wonders whom Landesman is really arguing with. For Quine didn't quite say that particular quantification all by itself creates or imposes ontological commitments. What he said was something like this: "You build yourself a nice theory of the universe and you write it down in canonical notation. And then you ask what must be in the domain of interpretation in order that the sentences of your theory come out true. And that will tell you what the ontology of the theory is. And if the theory is the best you can find, then you've got the most you can get by way of an account of the ontology of the world." And this, it seems to me, is quite compatible with interpreting the quantifiers of the canonical notation in Landesman's "ontologically noncommittal" way. For it isn't that the quantifier somehow breeds entities *in vacuo*, but rather that certain *uses* of the quantifier *in medias res* codify, systematize, and reveal ontological commitments arising from quite distinct theoretical or philosophical bases. Read this way, in fact, I suspect that Landesman's noncommittal interpretation just *is* Quine's existential interpretation (they both contrast appropriately, for example, with Barcan-Marcus's substitution interpretation), and the fourth heresy is not so heretical after all. There remains, I guess, some residual squabble over the word 'exists', but I've quite lost track of just what it is. I would give Landesman the word 'exists', but Quine gave it to Wyman back in 1948 and, as far as I know, Wyman hasn't given it back yet. And that's about all I have to say about existence as a real predicate (the fifth heresy).

Now I have skipped a whole heresy (the third) and veered away from the topic of reference in this rambling discussion. So let's correct both defects. The third heresy, you will recall, was that the distinctive function of an act of referring is not that of picking out or identifying an object. The argument for this one again sort of slips past the "reality of language in linguistic action" theme and plunks us in the middle of a theory of *judgments* which, we are told, are "acts of asserting something to oneself." Now judgments, according to Landesman, may be "made in words or, at least, in verbal imagery" but they *need* have nothing to do with language at all. Whether linguistic or nonlinguistic, however, judgments do make use of reference. "In judgment, the act of referring is simply the way one is conscious of the object the judgment is about." Now I don't quite understand this remark, and particularly the phrase "the way one is conscious of the object," for I can't come up with any plausible candidates for different ways one *can* be conscious of an object, but let that pass. The point is supposed to be that, since one knows or is conscious of what one is making a judgment about, one doesn't need to pick it out or identify it to oneself. *That* can't be what referring is all about.

Now we might observe, parenthetically, that if judging can go on without language, and if referring is an aspect of judging, then it is difficult to see how we will find out all those important heretical truths about *referring* by stressing the artifactuality and conventionality of *language*. Like a good Humean, I judge that what is distinguishable is separable and what is separable is separate, and since, on Landesman's account, judging—and hence referring—is distinguishable and separable from any linguistic embodiment, it is separate, and we can learn nothing of the nature of reference from our studies of the nature of language. But this presupposes that I can make some sense of Landesman's theory of nonlinguistic judgment. Well, let's try.

He writes: "It can be sufficient for a judgment [that a rock is gray] that I form a visual image of the gray rock in an assertive frame of mind." When I read that, I resolved to try the experiment. I first got myself into an assertive frame of mind. I did this by listening to a George Wallace campaign speech, watching two John Wayne movies, and reading the collected works of Gustav Bergmann. Then I formed a mental image of a gray rock on my front lawn. And be darned if I didn't immediately start making judgments! My first judgment was that the whole thing wasn't going to work. So I beefed up my mental image and found myself judging that the rock *could be* gray; then that it was probably gray; then that the image, at least, was gray; then that the rock wasn't all *that* gray; and finally, that the rock wasn't really gray at all, but sort of blue. But I couldn't get up a mental image of that, so I quit.

The moral of this story can be found in Part I of the *Philosophical Investigations*. Mental imagery and "an assertive frame of mind" may be characteristic *accompaniments* of some or all judgments, but it cannot be these things in which the judgments *consist*. This is by now an old story, and, in any case, I certainly haven't the time to tell it here. So I won't. I will say that, however ill I understand judgments, I understand Landesman's ventures into this swamp even less. I am convinced that if we can ever achieve an understanding of the diaphanous unspoken judgment, it will be by the light of linguistic analogy. And that being so, we must be especially wary of extinguishing the flickering candle of our linguistic understandings by such a too-precipitous plunge into the gloomy miasma of the mental.

Now where does this leave us? One heresy to go and Humpty Dumpty to be put back together again. About the sixth heresy—that logical predicates are referring expressions—I shall not have anything to say. We have already opened enough boxes to leave Pandora rolling in the aisles, but the problem of universals is one too many even for my venturesome tastes today. The prudent course seems to be to postpone the sixth heresy until we achieve some understanding of what it is for a logical *subject* to be a referring expression. Then, at least, we will know better what is at stake in awarding that honorific to the predicate as well. I know you were expecting Bradley's Regress again, but for the moment you'll have to settle for Rosenberg's Egress.

And now we must have a look at Humpty Dumpty. Our puzzles are puzzles only if reference is a relation between words and the world. Is reference a relation? Well, Landesman writes that

> it is necessary to distinguish those concepts that are required in order to interpret human discourse as discourse from those that designate particular de facto relations that bits of discourse bear to bits of the real world (p. 109).

And he gives us a nice collection of heresies which begin to make much better sense once we start playing with the notion that

reference *isn't* a word-object relation at all. But there's a ghost
in his machine. You can hear the lingering echoes of its voice:

> It is conceded that words acquire their referential connections
> to the world as a result of what people do with them (p. 105).

> . . . words acquire their referential connections to objects in
> the world through human action (p. 106).

This, recall, is the insight we are to take seriously. But such
talk of "referential connections" is deadly. For it all comes
back to roost. How can there be *connections* between a nice
solid word, say 'Pegasus', and something that doesn't exist at
all?

Look at the other term of the analysis: *actions.* What actions?
Well, what we're told is *"linguistic* actions", and as a paradigm
we get the action of *referring to an object* (or mentioning one,
or speaking of one). "Referring as an action, as something that
people do, is prior in the order of explanation to reference as a
semantic relation between a word and an object." Now I have
a heresy of my own. I deny that. The analysis runs the other
way. To perform the act of referring to X just *is* to deploy a
bit of language (or something quite like a bit of language) which
refers to X.

Does that put me back in the garden with Adam's Berlitz
lessons? Not at all. For I do *not* deny that linguistic reality is
conventional and that conventions are the products of human
action. What I *do* deny is that the actions in question are to be
described as *linguistic* actions—referring to X, predicating F of
a, saying that p, and so on. If we are going to take Humpty
Dumpty seriously, let's take him *seriously.* Agentizing our
semantics can't do that. That way lies only sterility. And I
can prove it.

How do I perform the act of referring to a thing? How do I—
how does *anyone*—use a word to refer to a thing? Well, try a
Grice-Searle line. It's typical. (It has to be typical; it's the only
proposal forthcoming.) I *intend* that my utterance of the word
will pick out the thing for the hearer. But how do I intend that
it is *that thing* (and not some other) which my utterance is to
pick out? How do I get that thing into my intending? And what
is it for the hearer to *pick out* the thing which I intend? In what
is his picking out that thing (and not some other) to consist?
Well, perhaps I *think of* the thing, and, if communication is
successful, upon hearing my utterance so does he. All right,

how do I think of a thing? In what does my thinking of that thing (and not some other) consist? How does that thing get into my thinking?

At any step along this path, I believe there are only two directions in which we can go. The first of these is mad—but it is a common and venerable route, so we should at least mark it. It is the way of an ontology of modes of being. The thing has *objective being* in the thought. Or the thing *intentionally inexists* in the thought. Or . . . make up your own jargon. One and the same thing *existing* in both ordinary and extraordinary ways. Well, if you can make that creaky, rusted old machine go, more power to you. I make you a gift of it.

But what is the alternative? Well, surely, not the thing itself in the thought, but some *representative* of the thing. A mental something that stands for the thing. Or (why not come right out and say it) a mental something which *refers* to the thing—a "mental word." And here we are, back where we began. We wanted to analyze the putative semantic relation of reference in terms of an act of referring. But our attempt to understand what an act of referring could be has brought us right back to the ostensible relation, now, to be sure, shoved indoors as obtaining between a *mental* item and the world rather than a *verbal* item and the world. But we will not analyze our semantics any better by mentalizing it than be agentizing it. What we have to do is to give up *this* program entirely. It is fundamentally misconceived, and it is, in consequence, sterile.

And where lies fertile ground? Well, you are entitled to an answer, but space requires that it be brief, so I shall make it dogmatic.[2] Here are *my* two theses for the church door:

(1) Reference is *not* a relation between words and the world. In sentences of the form 'the word W refers to X', what stands in the X-place is as much *exhibited* ("mentioned," if you wish) as what goes in for the 'W'. And the idiom as a whole is a bit of *classifying* talk, fixing the place of the expression W in the linguistic network by means of the role *displayed* by 'X'.

(2) The linguistic network as a whole, though, *is* fitted to the world. Not, however, by *semantic* relations, but by *real* relations, obtaining *in extenso* between items in the world and bits of language as objects of this same natural order (tokens) by virtue of the regularities of human tokening behavior—extensionally conceived and extensionally described.

2. For the long, non-dogmatic, version see my *Linguistic Representation* (Dordrecht, Holland: D. Reidel Publishing Company, 1974).

It is, in other words, only *by* treating words as "merely one kind of thing among other kinds in the world" that we *can* take seriously the view that words acquire their *representational* (not referential) connection with the world through human action. And there is a nice, compact name for this view, too, by the way. It is called, you might have guessed, *the picture theory*. But I have pounded *that* drum quite enough on other occasions.

Charles Landesman

Professor Rosenberg notes that it was shortly after his discourse with Alice that Humpty Dumpty took his fall. But between the fall and his presentation of his theory of language, Humpty Dumpty, at Alice's request, undertook an interpretation of "Jabberwocky." Professor Rosenberg's remarks also present an interpretive problem. On the one hand he appears to agree with my main point, and if this is a thesis nailed to the church door, then he is playing Calvin to my Luther. But on the other hand, he says things which appear to be inconsistent with the main point. It is difficult to believe that Professor Rosenberg, or anyone else for that matter, would assert an explicit contradiction.

Although he agrees with my rejection of an existence condition for reference, he disapproves of how I arrive at it. His main objection is, in his own words, as follows: "The successful consummation of many human actions—conventional and nonconventional—depends essentially upon the satisfaction of conditions external to the beliefs, intentions, and behaviors of the agent. We need an argument to show that referring is not such an action and the existence of the object such an external condition." It was, of course, just my intention to supply such an argument with my allusions to the conventionality of discourse. Rosenberg thinks that his golf example undercuts the argument. Playing golf is an activity regulated by conventions that also presupposes the existence of golf equipment, a golf course, greens, holes, and the like. I think, however, that the example supports my argument. Consider the circumstances under which the conventions of golf are communicated to the learner; in these circumstances the existence conditions are communicated as well: "Here is a golf club; there is the hole," and so on. Human language is unlike golf in just this respect—in the course of teaching someone how to talk about a field of objects, there is no requirement in general that the objects exist and no such requirement is communicated or implied. I suppose that, if one were wedded to an existence condition, one could just refuse to mention nonexistent objects and encourage others to do so as well. In that case, one's speech would fit the golf analogy. But, as a matter of fact, language isn't like that at all; it depends upon conventions in a more exclusive way than does something like golf.

Rosenberg's way of dispensing with the existence condition is simpler. He writes: "We *do* refer to lots of things that don't exist, and from this it follows that we *can.*" One wonders why, if things are that simple, the existence condition has been so widely accepted. How can one overlook such an evident fact? The answer is obviously that for those who accept the condition, that we do refer to lots of things that don't exist is not an evident fact at all. And the reason it is not evident is that the existence condition is thought to be required by various theories about language, theories, for example, about how words relate to the world. And the only way to argue against the condition is to provide an alternative theory, something that the *"ab esse, ad posse"* argument fails to do, even though it has the authority of scholasticism behind it.

Rosenberg does mention a type of case that I did not discuss except by implication. Does the subject phrase in "The tallest building in my living room is made entirely of polished Carrara marble" refer to anything? As Rosenberg notes, the famous examples of "the golden mountain" and "the present king of France" would do just as well. His example illustrates one of the major defects in standard discussions of reference. Examples of a fantastic sort are arbitrarily constructed with no context provided even to understand what is being said. One thus deals with mere sentences, not sentences used in linguistic actions. But mere sentences do not, qua sentences, contain phrases that refer, for mere phrases, in abstraction from human action, simply do not refer. Suppose someone says, "The present king of France is bald," intending to make a statement. What are we to make of this? Suppose the speaker has been reading a novel in which a bald character has just ascended the throne of France. Then what he says may well be true. Or suppose he sees a bald person whom he mistakenly believes to be the current ruler of France. Then again he said something that was true, although something that he said or implied was false. In these cases, there is something being referred to. If reference has no existence condition, it obviously has a subsistence condition: of anything referred to we can obviously say that there is such a thing. I will leave it to Professor Rosenberg to provide a plausible context for his use of "the tallest building in my living room"; after all, it is his living room.

It is, I suppose, possible to violate even the subsistence condition. If someone seriously says, "Hamlet's wife was a blonde," and if he does not mistakenly think that Ophelia or anyone else was wedded to Hamlet, then we can say to him that there is no such thing as Hamlet's wife, meaning not merely that such a thing does not exist, but that there is no such character in the play. Of course, a blonde wife of Hamlet is a creature of a logically possible world, and if that world happens to be the universe of discourse, then what was said turns out to be true. Where the subsistence condition is violated I would agree with Rosenberg that it is difficult to bring these cases into the true-false line of work.

Professor Rosenberg raises another sort of issue when he writes: "If judging can go on without language, and if referring is an aspect of judging, then it is difficult to see how we will find out all those important heretical truths about *referring* by stressing the artifactuality and conventionality of *language*." I never said that conventionality was necessary for reference. My essay aimed at certain targets, namely those discussions of reference *in language* which argued for an existence condition. Incidentally the sermon based upon a text of Wittgenstein was, as is usual with such sermons, tedious. And the sermon was directed at a straw man. A mere mental image is not, of course, a judgment, any more than a word is an assertion. But a mental act, analogous to a speech act, in which a mental image is used in a way analogous to a noun phrase can be a judgment. I am afraid that I encouraged the sermon by not being explicit enough.

I come now to what appears to be a basic contradiction in Professor Rosenberg's views. He asks: "Is reference a relation?" and offers, as his answer, this rhetorical question: "How can there be *connections* between a nice solid word, say 'Pegasus', and something that doesn't exist at all?" I was surprised by this, because, although we differed in points of detail, I though we agreed on the main point in rejecting an existence condition. Consider the true statements " 'Pegasus' refers to (is used to refer to) Pegasus" and "There is something that 'Pegasus' refers to." In my view these are both relational statements asserting a connection between something that does exist and something that does not. It is not uncommon in discussions of reference for it to be denied that these are relational. The reason for the denials is usually the acceptance of an existence condition. But if one does not accept the condition, then there is no harm in saying that there can be relations between things that do and things that do not exist, or between things that don't exist, as well as between things that do exist. Professor Rosenberg seems to be thinking in terms of the very existence condition he earlier rejected.

Here is a sample of his reasoning: "Reference is *not* a relation between words and the world. In sentences of the form 'the word W refers to X', what stands in the X-place is as much *exhibited* . . . as what goes in for the 'W'. And the idiom as a whole is a bit of *classifying* talk, fixing the place of the expression W in the linguistic network by means of the role *displayed* by 'X'." However, that such sentences classify the words that take the place of 'W' is not at all incompatible with their being of relational form. The sentence "John is the father of Tom" classifies John as a father as well as asserts a relation between John and Tom. And that the word which takes the place of 'X' is, in some sense, exhibited does not preclude the possibility of its also being used to refer; consider, for example, a literal exhibit of a Greek manuscript one of whose words refers to Pegasus. In fact it is not at all clear how sentences of the form "W refers to X" could explain the specific function of 'W' and distinguish it from the specific function of other referring expressions without telling which object it can be used to refer to. Rosenberg's account of sentences of these types is compatible with my view that reference is a relation.

In conclusion I would like to take up two points that were mentioned in the discussion that followed our papers. It was mentioned that I might be required to accept "The round square is round" as being a truth about the subsistent round square. I do not think so. The supposition that there is something that is both round and square is a necessary falsehood. Thus there is nothing and cannot be anything which "the round square" refers to. The denial of the existence condition does not lead to an ontology of impossibles. In fact, if I am correct, it does not lead to any ontology at all.

In passing I said that statements are used to refer to states of affiars. There was an objection, in the name of argument, which Donald Davidson has used. It goes like this. Let S and R be any distinct sentences with the same truth value. Consider now the following:

(1) R
(2) $\hat{x}(x = x.R) = \hat{x}(x = x)$
(3) $\hat{x}(x = x.S) = \hat{x}(x = x)$
(4) S

Now (1) is logically equivalent to (2), and (3) is logically equivalent to (4). If sentences refer to states of affairs, then (1) and (2) refer to the same state of affairs, and so do (3) and (4). Now the terms "$x(x = x.R)$" and "$x(x = x.S)$" have the same reference, and since (2) differs from (3) only in respect to terms having the same reference, they both refer to the same state of affairs. But then both R and S refer to the same state of affairs. Thus we have proved that all true sentences have the same reference, and all false sentences have the same reference. But, on the assumption that referents are state of affairs, then this is absurd, since any ontology of states of affairs would claim that there are more than two of them. I will not discuss whether, assuming the argument to be a good one, there is any absurdity here. I simply find implausible a presupposition of the argument that if sentences refer to states of affairs, then logically equivalent sentences refer to the same state of affairs. For this entails that the fact that seven plus five equals twelve is the very same fact as that the shortest distance between two points is a straight line. And that I find absurd.

ILLOCUTIONARY SUICIDE

Zeno Vendler

For the purposes of this paper I shall assume that the grammatical criteria I recently proposed for the recognition of illocutionary verbs (which, till we become wiser, I shall call performatives) are indeed correct.[1] Accordingly, I claim that the following marks constitute jointly sufficient conditions:

(a) Performatives are container verbs; that is, they require nominalized sentences for verb-objects. This feature distinguishes them from such ordinary transitives as *kick* or *push*.

(b) The verb-objects have to be imperfectly nominalized sentences ("factive" nominals in Lees's terms[2]) to distinguish the performatives from such container verbs as *watch* or *imitate*, which require perfectly nominalized sentences ("action" nominals to Lees). This feature is connected with the fact that the performatives, unlike these verbs, do not normally admit progressive tenses.

(c) The subject-slot is open exclusively to "human" noun phrases, which is not true of some other verbs displaying the previous marks, for example, *indicate, entail*, and so on.

(d) Performatives are achievement verbs according to their time-schema, unlike such state-verbs as *believe* or *intend*.[3]

(e) Finally, they characteristically occur in the first person singular present indicative active form (Austin's mark). This is not the case with some nonperformatives, such as *decide* and *find out*, which conform to all the previous criteria.

As we know, Austin has divided the illocutionary forces into five classes: expositives, verdictives, commissives, exercitives, and behabitives.[4] I tried to show, in the same publications, that this intuitive classification, with some extensions and refine-

1. By the author, "Say What You Think," in *Studies in Thought and Language*, ed. J. L. Cowan (Tucson: University of Arizona Press, 1970), pp. 79–97; idem, "Les performatifs en perspective," *Langages* 17 (1970): 73–90; idem, *Res Cogitans* (Ithaca, N.Y.: Cornell University Press, 1972).

2. R. B. Lees, *The Grammar of English Nominalizations* (The Hague: Mouton, 1960).

3. These notions are elaborated in chapter 4 of my *Linguistics in Philosophy* (Ithaca, N.Y.: Cornell University Press, 1967).

4. J. L. Austin, *How to Do Things with Words* (Oxford: Clarendon, 1962), Lecture XII, pp. 147–63.

ments, corresponds to a subdivision of performative verbs based upon their various syntactical constraints. A general idea, if not the details, of this subdivision will be relevant to our present investigations.

The semantic coherence of the class of performatives can be shown by invoking the "formulas" Austin uses to introduce the notion of a performative. These are the following:[5]

(a) *To say* "I V +" is to V +
(b) *In saying* "I V +" he V-ed +
(c) *I hereby V +*

We find that the verbs comfortably fitting into these formulas are more or less the same as the ones singled out by our joint syntactical criteria.

In addition, it is intuitively obvious that the variety of performatives displays the various ways of saying something, or, what amounts to the same thing, that the verb *say*, at least in its dominant sense, is a general performative. If proof is needed, consider the possible answers to the question "What did he say?" Any one of the following will do: "He stated that . . ." (an expositive), "He called me . . ." (a verdictive), "He promised to . . ." (a commissive), "He ordered me to . . ." (an exercitive), "He apologized for . . ." (a behabitive). Notice, however, that the verb *say* has a weaker sense too. One can "say" single words, sentences, rigmaroles, tonguetwisters, nonsense syllables, and so forth, without performing any illocutionary act. But in this case the answer to the question "What did he say?" has to repeat the original utterance word by word, or, as the case may be, phoneme by phoneme. In the sense of *say*, however, in which it is a general performative, that question is normally answered by an indirect quotation, which more often than not requires, and always allows, some indexical, lexical, and syntactical changes in the utterance reproduced. It appears, in fact, that saying something in the strong sense entails a license to reproduce indirectly. Hereafter I shall be concerned with saying in the strong sense only.

Remember, finally, that the domain of performatives is to be kept distinct from the domain of "perlocutionary" verbs. Just to refresh our memory, consider the difference, for instance, between the illocutionary *argue* and *warn*, and the perlocutionary *convince* and *deter*. Whereas the former are "pure" saying words, that is, they merely serve to describe what the speaker

5. V + represents the verb plus its verb-object.

does, the use of the latter also implies the appropriate compliance by the hearer. One can argue, yet fail to convince his audience, that something is the case, and one can warn another not to do a thing, without succeeding in deterring him from doing it. These few remarks should be sufficient to give content to my claim that the following discussion will not involve the perlocutionary dimension at all.

So far so good. It looks as if we have a fairly clear understanding of the performative domain. Unfortunately, as usually happens in linguistics, not to mention philosophy, we soon discern a fly in the ointment, or, rather, a swarm of tiny gnats. There is a quaint little group of verbs that, on the one hand, are obviously verbs of saying, yet, on the other, fail to show the Austinian mark, that is to say, they do not occur in the first person singular present tense at all. This, at the first blush, sounds unbelievable: verbs of saying that cannot be used in saying something. Yet there are such queer birds. Just to begin with, I mention a few, and to rub in the point, I even suggest the performative class to which they would belong were it not for this single shortcoming. Take *allege, insinuate* and *brag:* these look like expositives. *Egg on, goad, incite* and *threaten* are similar to the exercitives. Finally, some quasi-behabitives: *scold, berate, scoff* and *flatter.*

Let us go into some details. To say, for instance, that Joe alleged or insinuated something, or that he bragged about this or that, is to report on some "expositive" speech acts he performed, no less than to say, for example, that he asserted or suggested something, or that he informed us about this or that. Similarly, I can describe some of Joe's "exercitive" speech acts by saying that he ordered or begged me to do, or warned me not to do, something or other, as well as by saying that he egged me on or incited me to do, or threatened me with something to deter me from doing, such and such. Again, as I can tell you what he said "behabitively" by reporting that he blamed, praised or condemned me, so can I do the same thing by reporting that he scolded, berated, taunted or upbraided me.

These observations, moreover, are no mere impressions; they are based on linguistic facts. For the question we employed before, "What did he say?", can be answered by using these verbs as much as the true performatives. "What did he say?" "Well, [we may answer] he alleged . . ., bragged . . ., threatened . . ., taunted . . ., scolded . . .," and so forth. Yet, and this is the rub, no one can allege anything in saying "I allege

. . .," no one can insinuate in saying "I insinuate . . .," no one can incite in saying "I incite . . .," no one can threaten in saying "I threaten . . .," and no one can scold in saying "I scold . . . ." In fact, except for the irrelevant "habitual" present, we do not use these verbs in the first person singular present form at all, which form is said to be the primary and most characteristic one for all real performatives. We cannot escape the conclusion: these verbs are verbs of saying, yet not performatives.

Why is this so? In other words, what goes wrong in trying to use these verbs in the performative way? This is the question to which I shall address myself below. Such an investigation may appear trivial to the uninitiated. To us, however, who remember the results of Austin's study of illocutionary "infelicities," it comes naturally to expect to learn more from cases where things go wrong than from cases where they run smoothly on schedule. As the "doctrine of infelicities" has engendered the doctrine of presuppositions, so I hope to derive from the present study some worthy offspring pertaining to the semantics of the performatives, in other words, to the idea of what it is to say something. Gnats are less important than elephants, yet the study of gnats may reveal more about the nature of life than will the study of elephants.

I begin the detail work with the group of quasi-expositives. First, to have more specimens, I add pairs to the ones already mentioned: *brag* reminds one of the milder *boast, insinuate* the nicer *hint*, and *allege* evokes the worse, and very important, *lie*.

Why is it, then, that although it may be true that Joe has alleged that he had met Howard Hughes, he could not have made this claim by saying "I (hereby) allege that I have met Howard Hughes"? Well, for one thing, because no one would believe him—you opine. But—I reply—what has this got to do with the health of his speech act? Suppose I were to claim, despite the Apollo missions, that the moon was made of green cheese. Certainly nobody would believe me, to be sure, but this universal incredulity would not vitiate the soundness of my speech act, and would not prevent me from making the performative work; to say (in the appropriate circumstances) "I claim that the moon is made of green cheese" is to make a silly claim, but a claim nevertheless. On the contrary, not even concerning matters which are quite believable can I succeed in alleging something by saying, for instance, "I allege that I met your wife yesterday."

The reason why people would not believe me if I started my utterance with "I allege" does not lie in what follows these words, but in the use of this very phrase. By saying "I allege," I would cast doubt upon what I intended to allege. But—one might object—there need not be anything wrong with such a move. After all, the point of saying, for instance, "I guess" or even "I suggest," rather than "I state" or "I maintain," is precisely to allow some shadow of doubt to creep upon the truth of what I say. If this is acceptable with *guess*, why not with *allege*?

Let us try another tack. What, exactly, do I mean when I say, in the past tense, that Joe (or you or I, for that matter) has alleged that p? The answer is easy: by using this word I indicate that he asserted (not just guessed or suggested) that p, but to me p appears to be false or dubious. But then, once more, why cannot Joe himself do his alleging by employing this very word? What prevents him from asserting that p and adding that it is, or at least might be, false? The answer is that asserting that p is not compatible with a concurrent admission that p might be dubious or false.

What do I do when I assert that p? I claim your belief for p, I call upon you to believe that p, because I say so.[6] Then, of course, I cannot destroy with my left what I build with my right: I cannot ask you to take my word for p while adding that in my opinion it is unworthy of belief. And this is exactly what the performative use of *I allege* would do. Therefore I cannot possibly allege that p in saying "I allege that p;" to do so would amount to an illocutionary suicide.

In order to facilitate subsequent discussion, I introduce here the notion of an "illocutionary aim." The illocutionary aim of a speech act is the mental act, or the mental state, the speaker intends the listener to perform or to adopt. Thus, for example, if I say to you "I will be there," and I merely intend you to believe this, then the act I perform is a statement or a forecast. If, in addition, I want you to come to rely on my word, then it is a promise. Finally, if my intention is to provoke your fear of my going there (because, perhaps, you are planning to denounce me there, or some such thing), then it is a warning. In most cases my intention can be discerned from context and circumstance. If these are not clear enough, or if I want to be sure of the uptake, then I use the explicit performative: *state,*

6. Here I make use of H. P. Grice's theory of meaning. See his "Meaning," *Philosophical Review* 66 (1957): 377–88.

promise, or *warn*. And you, if you fully understand me, will
know what illocutionary aim I intended to achieve. Whether
or not you in fact will come to believe, rely upon, or fear my
going there is as irrelevant to the uptake of the message, that
is, to the understanding of what I said, as the overt actions you
might perform as a result.

In these terms, when I say that Joe has alleged that *p*, what
I mean is, first, that *his* illocutionary aim in saying that *p* was
to make his audience believe that *p*, and, second, that in *my*
opinion *p* is dubious. In such a nonperformative context these
two aspects do not clash. They would, however, as we just saw,
in the performative case: the illocutionary aim implied by the
use of the word *allege* would be frustrated by the operation
of the second factor. Consequently Joe, if he uses an explicit
performative in making his allegation, must select a bona fide
performative (such as *state* or *claim*), which, on the one hand,
expresses the same illocutionary aim, namely, evoking belief,
but, on the other, does not have the second feature (I shall call
it the "spoiling factor") undermining that very aim.

Given the notions of illocutionary aim and spoiling factor,
it is not at all difficult to see what is the trouble with the
performative use of the other quasi-expositives we mentioned
above. In the case of *lie*, the illocutionary aim is the same; the
liar, no less than the "stater" and the "alleger," wants to be
believed. The spoiling factor is of the same kind as the one with
allege, only stronger. To say that Joe lied that *p* is to imply that
he knew *p* to be false. Therefore, Joe could not possibly preface
his lie by saying "I lie." *Lying*, as I said, is an important word,
and I shall return to it toward the end. Here I merely mention
a closely related verb, *slander;* this, of course, means lying about
other people to their detriment, and consequently the already
strong spoiling factor of *lie* is further increased.

Insinuate and *hint* present a different and more complicated
picture. What do I mean when I say that Joe insinuated that
something was the case, or hinted at something being the case?
Well, once more, he intended to create a belief, but he went
about it in a roundabout and devious manner. Suppose Joe
says to Jim, "Is your wife still working for John? I see them
having lunch together every day." Their having lunch together
every day has a certain prima facie implication, but Joe, who
is not merely implying but insinuating, seemingly thwarts this
implication by mentioning another possibility: her working for
John. Had Joe not added this, Jim might have asked back "What

do you imply?'', and Joe, if he had the courage, might have
answered back, "I imply [notice the performative] that John
and your wife . . .," and so forth. As it is, he does not want to
provoke Jim, and so, as it were, he acts stupid; he pretends not
to be aware of the implication himself. Thus we see that the
illocutionary aim of insinuation is belief all right, to be more
exact belief resulting from an inference, but this aim is hidden
behind a disguise masking the speaker's true intentions. This
last feature, obviously, constitutes the spoiling factor with respect to performative employment: no one can insinuate anything in saying "I insinuate . . . ;" it would let the cat out of
the bag.

With hinting, if I understand it correctly, the spoiling factor
is weaker: one does not positively disguise one's aim, only
leaves it to the audience to divine it, that is, to take the hint.
Even *imply* has a mild spoiling factor: one cannot begin the
conversation by saying "I imply . . . ."

Now what about *brag*, and its weaker sister *boast?* In the
light of the previous, it is easy to account for the performative
failure of *brag* and, on a minor scale, of *boast.* When we say
that the braggart brags, or the boaster boasts, we mean that he
intends to inform or remind us in his speech act of some of his
real or imagined qualities, achievements, or possessions, with
the added aim of provoking admiration or envy, which, in our
estimation, he does not deserve. This last feature, of course, is
the spoiling factor, the existence of which prevents the braggart
from saying "I brag" in his braggings. As to *boast*, the "spoiler"
is quite weak (we are not sure whether he really deserves our
admiration), and so, with some misgivings, one might say "I
boast . . ." and boast, as St. Paul does in 2 Cor. 11: "I say again,
Let no man think me a fool; if otherwise, yet as a fool receive
me, that I may boast myself a little. . . . Are they Hebrews?
So am I. . . . Are they ministers of Christ? (I speak as a fool)
I am more." In any case, boasting or bragging is against due
modesty, and so it tends to diminish the very effect the boaster
and the bragger wish to achieve. This aspect, of course, enhances
the spoiling factor mentioned above.

Before closing our discussion on the quasi-expositives I mention one more, *blurt out.* Blurting out a secret is distinct from,
say, revealing or betraying a secret. These last two acts are
intentional: the traitor tells his tale being aware that it is a
secret. This is not so with blurting out: in a real case of blurting
out the speaker does not know, or momentarily forgets, that

what he tells is a secret, which he is not supposed to reveal. To say, therefore, "I blurt out . . ." would be something like saying "I am going to tell you something I should not, but I am not aware that I should not." And this would be another illocutionary suicide.

Turning to quasi-exercitives, I give a fuller list than I did before. One feels that *egg on* and *goad* are similar in meaning, while *incite* and *instigate* fall into another class, and *threaten* stands alone. The first two, incidentally, are to be distinguished from their perlocutionary cousins, to wit, *entice, seduce* and, perhaps, *cajole.*

The performative use of *egg on* and *goad* would fail as *hint* and *insinuate* fail in this respect. Here, of course, the illocutionary aim is different: as with all exercitives, the listener is supposed to gather that he is called upon to do something, not just to believe something. Now the egger and the goader, as much as the hinter and the insinuator, have these aims, but do not reveal them, and often try to dissimulate. "You could not do it, Charlie, could you? . . . You just don't have the guts. . . . Joe did it, but he is a real man . . . ." This is how goading and egging go: the speaker wants his victim to do something, and usually something silly at that, but he does not ask him outright—he tells him things that are apt to provoke him to do the foolish act. It is due to this spoiling factor that the speaker could not possibly say "I egg you on to . . ." or "I goad you into . . ." and be egging or goading.

Incite and *instigate* do not fail on the account of honesty, but of something else. If I say that Joe incited violence or instigated murder, I imply that what he wanted to bring about was—at least to my mind—wrong or undesirable, that is, that it should not take place. Then the performative conflict is easy to see: in saying, for instance, "I incite you to do *x*" I would say, on the one hand, that I want you to do *x*, yet, on the other, that I think it ought not be done.

Finally *threaten.* As I said above, it is similar to *warn*, at least to the exercitive *warn* ("I warn you not to do *x*"), which is different from the expositive *warn* ("The bull is going to charge"). Yet I can say "I warn . . ." in warning, but I cannot say "I threaten . . ." in threatening. Why is this so? What is the spoiling factor? It is a subtle one. If I describe what somebody said as a warning, I do not imply that what he did was morally untoward, but if I describe it as a threat, I normally do. What I mean in this second case is that the speaker has exerted undue influence over his victim. If so, then I cannot threaten in saying

"I threaten," because by using this verb I would invite you to disregard my threat, since it constitutes coercion that ought to be resisted.

The little gnats swarm in the behabitive domain. They are rarely used verbs, and so their semantic structure is often unclear. Yet they seem to fall into two groups: *scold, berate, nag,* and *upbraid* are typical members of the first, and *scoff, mock, taunt, gibe, jeer,* and *belittle,* and the opposite *flatter,* seem to belong to the second. They all appear to have derogatory connotations; the first group indicates something wrong with the performance: rudeness, repetition, exaggeration, and the like. The trouble with the second group goes deeper: in using these terms we indicate that the speaker's words are undeserved—that the victim of scoffing does not deserve the slight, and the object of flattery does not deserve the praise, perhaps not even in the scoffer's or flatterer's own opinion.

Remember that the illocutionary aim of a behabitive speech act is to convey the speaker's attitude towards the addressee's deeds or qualities: praise, blame, gratitude, resentment, and the like. This feature, of course, is incompatible with the implication of undeservedness, which is the spoiling factor of the second group. Thus to scoff in saying "I scoff at you . . ." or to flatter in saying "I flatter you . . ." would be self-destructive.

But how does the spoiling factor operate with the first group? Why cannot I scold or berate somebody by using these very verbs? The only reason I can think of is that by explicitly admitting the bad manners and the exaggeration these words allude to, I would diminish my moral authority to blame. Thus if I were to prefix my scolding or berating by "I scold (or berate) . . ." I would, as it were, allow you to belittle my blame as coming from an unworthy source, or at least in an improper garb. After all, as I can reject an assertion by saying "Who are you to claim that?", meaning that you are an ignoramus; as I can reject an order by saying "Who are you to order me about?", meaning that you have no authority; so I can reject your censure by saying "Who are you to blame me?", meaning that you lack the moral stature to do so.

We can best summarize the upshot of our survey by suggesting an alternative to Austin's approach to illocutionary verbs. To him, as his tests show, the primary and paradigmatic occurrence of such a verb is in the performative frame—the first person present. Hence he is bound to miss the little group we just discussed. My proposal is this: let us assume that the "original" use of all saying words has been the descriptive rather than the performative one. Let us assume, in other words, that "originally" (and I do not necessarily mean historical priority)[7] people used such verbs to report other people's speech acts. Accordingly, the meaning of these verbs is constructed out of a variety of semantic elements characterizing those speech acts on various levels: specification of illocutionary aim (think of the difference between stating, ordering, and apologizing); manner of performance (think of the difference between affirming and insisting, or between demanding, asking, and begging); the reporter's own opinion concerning either the content or the manner of the original speech act (think of the difference between stating and alleging, between praising and flattering, between boasting, bragging, and crowing); and so forth. Now most of these saying verbs are such that their semantic structure does not prevent their performative use, simply because it contains no factor that would frustrate the illocutionary aim of the speaker. Thus it is understandable—to use a historical model—that people might have felt inclined to employ this arsenal of verbs to make their aims explicit in their own speech acts. In this way, most of the saying verbs, "illocutionary" verbs, became performatives. The small class we discussed, then, represent the remainder which, owing to a spoiling factor in their semantic structure, could not make the grade.

Having told the truth, I return to *lying*, which, as I said, is a very important verb. The main conclusion is this: one cannot lie in saying "I lie . . ." because doing so would be claiming credence for something explicitly labelled as false. If I use *lie*, the spoiling of the speech act is done by the verb itself. Can it be done by other means? Undoubtedly, but it may take longer breath. Some examples:

It is raining, but this is false.
It is raining, but don't believe it.
It is raining, but I don't believe it.

This last, of course, is Moore's paradox. Its solution, given our theory, is clear: I ask someone to believe that *p* because I say so, adding that I myself don't believe it. Then why should he?

What goes wrong in these expositive cases can be parallelled in other illocutionary domains. Some examples:

I order you to go, but please don't.

7. Austin himself indulges in similar historical speculations: *How to Do Things with Words*, pp. 71–73.

I give you this house, but it is not mine.
I declare you man and wife, but I have no authority.

and so forth. The use of a wrong saying verb is not the only way
of committing illocutionary suicide; there are other weapons.

Moore's paradox reminds us of the ancient and venerable
Paradox of the Liar. Suppose I utter "What I am saying now is
false." Is this true or false? This what? "This sentence" will not
do, since sentences are not true or false, particularly not sentences studded with indexicals, as this is. "This statement" is
no good either, since the illocutionary aim of stating, creating
belief, is explicitly thwarted by the speaker himself. He could
not have even lied in saying this, since lying has the same aim.
Consequently the speaker did not say (in the strong sense)
anything in saying (in the weak sense) what he said. And since
in the relevant sense he did not say anything, there is nothing
that could be true or false. If I pretend to give you a house that
does not belong to me, my gift is neither generous nor stingy—
there is no gift.

Finally, when the Cretan said, "All Cretans are liars," meaning
that each and every statement made by a Cretan in the past and
in the future is intentionally false, then he could not have included that very statement, under the penalty of breaking its
assertive (or belief-claiming) force, that is, of spoiling it as a
statement. It is possible, therefore, that what he said was true
(if the Cretans were indeed such a mendacious lot). In that
case, however, any other statement to the effect that all Cretans
are liars, in the given sense, would be false, since our Cretan has
made a true statement.

If you ask, "But what about *the* statement that all Cretans
are liars?", I reply that there is no such thing *in abstracto*. Statements belong to persons, they are *their* statements made at a
certain time. Consequently, from the point of view of the natural language, we do not have to worry about written "statements" accusing one another of falsity from opposite boxes on
a piece of paper. They are no statements, they have no illocutionary force; no person stands behind them. If there is—say,
if I write them down and hand the paper to you to peruse—even
then they will be no statements but material evidence of an
illocutionary suicide.

Within a formal system, of course, the paradox may arise, and
may have to be eliminated by equally formal means such as the
introduction of metalanguages. The natural language, however,
is free of this trouble.

COMMENTS

Charles E. Caton

Vendler states five conditions, numbered (a) to (e), which, he holds, jointly suffice to class a verb fulfilling them as a *performative* (or *illocutionary*) *verb*, that is, one of the verbs which can be the main verb in an explicit performative utterance, in Austin's sense. One of Vendler's conditions is that

(e) they [i.e., the performative verbs] characteristically occur in the first person singular present indicative active form

which he terms *Austin's mark*. Vendler says that condition (e) is not satisfied by the verbs 'decide' and 'find out', although they satisfy all of the other four conditions. Now I don't know what Vendler means by saying of a verb that it "characteristically" occurs in a certain grammatical form. I do not think this notion of "characteristic" occurrence can be a statistical concept (and, if it is, it is probably not important to the matters Vendler is discussing). Of course performative verbs, *when being used to construct explicit performative utterances*, characteristically occur in the grammatical way in question; but Vendler would not, I think, want to give *this* explanation of the meaning of 'characteristically' in (e), since it involves the notion of an explicit performative utterance and he thinks that his set of jointly sufficient conditions can be stated purely syntactically. (I don't; see below.) A question is whether Vendler can *avoid* that circular-looking phrasing of condition (e).

Might we rephrase condition (e) by just dropping the word 'characteristically'? No, since most, if not all, verbs can "occur in the first person singular present indicative active form."[1] It appears later that Vendler means to include also the verb's being *noncontinuous* in (e); even so, most, if not all, verbs so occur, since they do so when laws, regularities, habits, customs, and so on are being stated—that is, they can occur in what is called the *habitual present* use. Even 'decide' and 'find out' can do so: "whenever she decides to go to a party, I decide not

1. Like Vendler, I have reference to the English language throughout.

147

to"; "whenever I overdraw, I find out that I have from my bank."

Note that Vendler needs a good statement of condition (e), because it is the failure of (e) and (e) only that defines his group of *quasi*-performative verbs. He says,

> there is a quaint little group of verbs that . . . are obviously verbs of saying, yet . . . fail to show the Austinian mark, that is . . ., they do not occur in the first person singular present tense at all.[2]

As stated, this is of course incorrect because of the habitual present, in which, as he later[3] correctly notes, these verbs occur. A better statement of (e) is, in effect, supplied by Vendler elsewhere[4] when he notes that the *performative present* use (as it may be called) does not admit of modification by certain temporal adverbs which *are* applicable to the habitual present.[5] Such adverbs include 'always' and 'often', which are obviously semantically consistent modifications of the habitual present but not of the performative present, which by its very nature admits as a temporal adverb[6] only 'now' (or ones to the same effect) and usually does not have one. The better statement of (e) that Vendler in effect supplies is thus something like

(e′)   *V* can occur, as a main verb, in the first-person non-continuous present indicative active modified by the temporal adverb 'now'

(where *V* is the verb in question).

Unfortunately, (e′) is only better, not adequate. The trouble is that we change habits, including speech habits. Suppose I never used to undertake to comment on papers but do do so *now:* I might have occasion then to say,

(1)   I never used to comment on papers. I undertake to do so now, though.

2. Z. Vendler, "Illocutionary Suicide," this volume, p. 137.
3. Ibid., p. 138.
4. Z. Vendler, "Say What You Think," in *Studies in Thought and Language,* ed. J. L. Cowan (Tucson: University of Arizona Press, 1970), p. 83.
5. Note that the surface forms (especially reduced conversational forms) of sentences involving the verb in the two uses may coincide, which makes it difficult to characterize the difference between the uses merely in terms of the surface forms.
6. The qualification 'temporal adverb' is necessary because of the sort of 'now' we have in 'Now, when Caesar crossed the Rubicon, he said . . .'.

That is, I may have meant that I now habitually do something I did not before, though of course, actually, the second sentence of (1) is ambiguous as to illocutionary force and could also have been a performative.[7]

It is also necessary to mention stage-direction talk, as when a director, not remembering, asks an actor about the action in a play, asking, "What do you do then?" The actor's answer can have to do with acts of saying and can use both performatives and quasi-performatives, as respectively in

(2) I tell her to go to a nunnery.   (performative)

and

(3) I insinuate that she remarried too soon after my father's death.   (quasi-performative)

I mention this use only for completeness and will call it the *stage-direction present*.

Note that because quasi-performative verbs occur in the habitual present and do so even in the first person,[8] there arises the possibility that a speaker might, using a quasi-performative *V* in this form, thereby *V*. In fact, I think this possibility is realized—that one might, for example, scold someone by saying what one habitually scolded. "I scold children when I find them with their hand in the cookie-jar," Granny might say, thereby scolding a child found in this compromising position. As far as I can see, this sort of thing could occur with each of the quasi-performative verbs Vendler mentions, so that he must rephrase points like "to scoff in saying 'I scoff at you . . .' or to flatter in saying 'I flatter you . . .' would be self-destructive";[9] so far from being self-destructive, it might be an especially forceful way of scolding a person to say what one habitually scolded people (or even just him) for, and similarly with the other quasi-performatives.

Now note that this present temporal adverb of the *habitual* use, 'now', is further temporally qualifiable in the usual ways of the habitual present, that is, with 'always', 'often', 'occasionally', 'never', and so on. Instead of the second sentence of

---

7. I believe it is possible to pronounce the string in such a way as to make clear how it is meant.

8. Vendler agrees in "Illocutionary Suicide," p. 138.

9. Ibid., p. 143. Remarks needing this sort of rephrasal, because they are incorrect if literally taken, occur on pp. 137–138, 141, 142, 143, and 144 ('I lie to the tax people every time' might be used to lie).

(1) we could have had any of

$$(4) \quad I \quad \left\{ \begin{array}{l} \text{always} \\ \text{often} \\ \text{occasionally} \\ \text{never} \\ \quad \textit{etc.} \end{array} \right. \quad \text{undertake to do so, now.}$$

still without turning the utterance into an explicit performative,
of course. But, notice, adding such temporal adverbs (whether
along with 'now' or not) will infallibly make the utterance
*non*performative. I see no alternative here except to appeal to
these semantic or illocutionary factors and to state condition
(e) in some such form as

(e″)   *V* can occur, as a main verb, in the first person non-
continuous present indicative active modified by the
temporal adverb 'now' in a sentence *S* such that, when
a further temporal adverb like 'always' or 'often'[10] is
added, the illocutionary force (or illocutionary-act
potential[11]) of *S* changes.

Note that in (e″) it would just be a question of the illocutionary
force of *S changing*, not of its changing from this to that (that
is, from a statement to a performative). The appeal to illocutionary force involved here would thus be like the appeal to
meaning in syntax or phonology, where it seems to suffice to
know that the meaning has changed, not how it has changed.
But I don't see how to avoid actually making this appeal here
to semantics (and/or, or including, illocutionary force), for
just referring to a change in the meaning of the *sentence* involved (as syntax is allowed to do) does not suffice: of *course*
adding 'always', 'occasionally', or similar words will in general
change the meaning of the sentence.[12] But if it changes a sentence fit for promising, say, into one not fit for promising, but
only for making statements about what one habitually promises,
then we have what is needed, for if the verb *V cannot* occur
as a main verb in such a way that the sentence in which it is
occurring can have its illocutionary force changed from that of
a performative to that of a nonperformative, then clearly either

10. I would assume this was a definable class of expressions (perhaps
not finite).
11. These terms must, then, be taken in a sense that abstracts from the
"propositional content"—a Searlean rather than an Alstonian sense.
12. Perhaps adding 'now' wouldn't.

it can't be performative in the first place or else it cannot *fail*
to be performative (can't change from being performative).
The former rules out *V* as a performative verb; and, as to the
latter, I think every performative verb (and possibly *every*
verb) can be used in the habitual present as well as in the performative present way. That is, I don't think there *are* any
verbs that cannot fail to be performative because they have only
a performative use.

In connection with the apparent fact that information that
is not merely syntactical seems to be required to state condition (e) properly, I note that it would bring Vendler's claim
that performative verbs can be purely syntactically characterized
into question. I would like to suggest, though, that this situation
is not necessarily disastrous. In fact, suppose we have no
definition or sufficient condition of a verb's being an illocutionary or performative verb. (As far as I know, this is the
case.) Then it might easily be of use to know what we might
call *amplifying conditions* (sufficient, necessary, or both), ones
the statement of which employs the explicandum concept in
both of the clauses joined by 'if', 'only if', or 'if and only if',
but which in one of the clauses so employs it as to amplify
upon its essential nature. For example, suppose that those
philosophers are right who have thought (incorrectly, in my
opinion) that one could really only refer to things that actually
existed; this view might perhaps be expressed as an amplifying
necessary condition by saying that

(5)   If one refers to something, one refers to it as existing.

If one didn't know this (assuming it to be correct), one could
learn something about referring from it, namely (of course)
that one cannot refer to something without referring to it as
existing. Many philosophical questions could, I think, be
regarded as questions so formulable as to be merely about
amplifying conditions.[13] I therefore think it might well be that
Vendler's (allegedly) jointly sufficient conditions for a verb
to be performative, in *my* version (e″), would still be useful
and interesting.

Since Vendler's statement of condition (e) is (even, as above,
on his own showing) deficient, I will, on the basis of the fore-

13. J. W. Meiland's book *Talking about Particulars* (London: Routledge
& Kegan Paul, 1970) issues in an analysis of referring which is only
amplifying, but it is I think interesting even so.

going discussion, take as the relevant definition of a quasi-performative verb the following:

(6)   *V* is a quasi-performative verb = df. *V* satisfies Vendler's conditions (a)–(d), but not the condition (e″).

Now, that Vendler has, as he says, located not just a fly but a "swarm of tiny gnats" in the healing ointment of Austin's General Theory of Speech Acts seems to me clear. They are *not*, perhaps, in Austin's Special Theory, in which Vendler's quasi-performatives would just be, crudely, lumped in with the constatives, since they aren't genuine performatives. The General Theory, though, states that an illocutionary force (or set of such, an illocutionary-act potential, Alston's terms[14]) attaches to every utterance in which a *l*ocutionary act has been performed. The locutionary level of description permits the definition of the grammatical term 'verb of saying', employed (but not defined) by Vendler: given a set of what may be termed *locutionary verbs*[15]—for instance, 'say (that)', 'ask (to)', 'ask (wh-)', 'tell (to)',[16]—a *verb of saying* can be explained thus:

(7)   *V* is a verb of saying = df. that some speaker *V*–ed + entails that he locuted +.[17]

where 'locuting' stands in for any of the various locutionary verbs and the complement (or "verb-object"), denoted by '+', is chosen appropriately, given a particular choice of the locutionary verb.

Then Vendler's "gnats" are verbs of saying which are not *genuine* performative verbs. Note that the fact of their existence relates to a doctrine of Austin's, namely the doctrine that (as he says[18]) "to perform a locutionary act is in general . . . also

14. W. P. Alston, *Philosophy of Language* (Englewood Cliffs, N. J.: Prentice-Hall, 1964), chap. 2.

15. As the linguist Georgia Green noted (in a talk at the University of Illinois Linguistics Seminar, entitled "How to Get People to Do Things with Words"), it is not always just the reporting verb of saying that is in question, but sometimes the phrasing of the complement clause (Vendler's "verb-object"), as, for example, in 'He told me I should go', which can report the direct discourse 'Go!' when 'He told me to go' cannot (quite as accurately, if at all).

16. Suggested by J. L. Austin's discussion on pp. 96–97 of *How to Do Things with Words* (Oxford: Oxford University Press, 1962).

17. '*V* +' is used in Vendler's way to denote the verb *V* plus a grammatically possible complement.

18. Austin, *How to Do Things with Words*, p. 98.

and *eo ipso* to perform an *illocutionary* act." For it is clear that Vendler's use of the traditional concept of a "verb of saying" can be taken, as suggested above, in a way consistent with Austin's views; and it is clear that Austin's illocutionary acts are those the names of which are provided by what Vendler calls "performative" and "illocutionary" verbs, except, according to Austin (apparently) but not Vendler, the *lo*cutionary verbs.[19] Vendler points out a decently large group of verbs of saying that are not performative verbs. They aren't because they don't satisfy condition (e)—(e″), really, I suggest—which was discussed above. That there are a number of "gnats" of this sort in the Austinian ointment I am, for my part, persuaded by what Vendler has said. It is, however, somewhat unclear why they are called "gnats" in the ointment: Austin's doctrine (just stated) could still hold, as long as there was *another* (specific) illocutionary verb for each given quasi-performative verb of saying. For example, if you *brag* you *say*, but you also *state*, and so Austin's doctrine that if you locute you illocute is still intact. Austin didn't say that whatever species of locuting described what a speaker did was a particular way of illocuting; it might[20] describe instead the *manner* of locuting or saying, for example.

I have two further difficulties in following Vendler's characterization of what this sort of "gnat" *is:* it is not clear to me that Vendler's account of how his quasi-performatives fail to be genuine performatives, that is, fail condition (e″), is correct in its specific details; and, more importantly, there seem to be *other* quasi-performatives, other verbs answering Vendler's description of quasi-performatives,[21] which pretty clearly can't be accounted for along his lines, that is, in terms of his notions of illocutionary aims and spoiling factors.

First, recall Vendler's basic line concerning the failure of quasi-performatives to have a performative use. It is outlined in terms of what he calls "illocutionary aims" and "spoiling factors." A *spoiling factor* for a quasi-performative *V* is a feature of its use which would, in the performative present (actually nonexistent), defeat the illocutionary aim of a *report* of the speech act *V* names. This *illocutionary aim* of a report of a

19. It seems to me Vendler and Searle (among others) are right in taking the locutionary verbs to be also illocutionary.

20. As Vendler notes, "Illocutionary Suicide," p. 144.

21. Cf. note 9 above.

speech act is "the mental act, or the mental state, the speaker intends the listener to perform or to adopt."[22] The basic line on quasi-performatives is, then, simply that the illocutionary aim of reports of them is such as would have a spoiling factor in the performative first person. For example, in saying someone *hinted*, one says he intended to convey something without actually saying that it was so; and so if 'hint' were a genuine performative (rather than the quasi-performative it in fact is)—if there were a performative utterance 'I (now/hereby) hint that p'—then in that utterance the speaker would be, in effect, saying that p with a verb ('hint') which, when predicated of a speaker (with respect to a content p), implies that he intended to convey that p *without* actually saying that p. There would be an obvious incoherence (though I guess a practical or "pragmatic" one) in such an act, which is the spoiling factor.[23]

Somewhere I feel I should note one peculiarity of Vendler's basic line on quasi-performatives, even though I can't think of anything further to do with it. Austin's quintessential observation about performative utterances was that they were not using words to *report* deeds, but rather to *perform* deeds. Vendler's line on quasi-performatives involves thinking (counterfactually) about the illocutionary aims of *reports* of them; by thinking about these, we see why they can't be *genuine* performatives. But the illocutionary aims of reports of them are incoherent only in the (actually nonexistent) performative first person, in which—assuming Austin's observation—those utterances would not have been *reports* at all. I sense that Vendler is asking us to consider an (actually nonexistent) utterance as both a *report* of a deed and also, at the same time, that very deed which would have been reported (had the performative utterance existed). *Can* any utterance be so viewed?

Since the verification of Vendler's line on quasi-performatives is a matter of what the details of usage are, and since I want to

22. Vendler, "Illocutionary Suicide," p. 139. I.e., the *standard* one for the speech act in question. Cf. H. P. Grice, agreeing, who uses the idea of such a standard intention systematically in his "Utterer's Meaning, Sentence Meaning, and Word Meaning," *Foundations of Language* 4 (1968): 1–18, and other writings.

23. Cf. Vendler, "Illocutionary Suicide," pp. 140–41. Given this description of the basic line, it is clear why Vendler relates it to the Moorean or "pragmatic" paradoxes and to the Liar Paradox.

claim that Vendler has gotten a number of those details wrong, I need at least to give some examples. Take 'allege':[24] dictionary accounts suggest that the connotation of 'allege' is not the *falsity* of what is alleged but rather its assertion *without proof*, that is, without evidence or support of some kind.[25] Not only is this detail about what 'allege' means wrong, but further, the *right* description does not fit in with Vendler's basic line on why quasi-performatives lack the performative first person: if the connotation were what Vendler alleges, then a performative use of 'I allege' would engender a Liar Paradox (one would be saying that what one was saying was false). But why shouldn't there be a performative use of 'I allege', when actually all that is connoted is, apparently, that no proof or supporting evidence for what is said is there and then being given? We say things without proof and without giving proof all the time, and why shouldn't we do so? And, if we do, why shouldn't we performatively say that that's what we're doing here and now, or say what connotes this?[26] Vendler's basic line can, as far as I can see, provide no answer here.

As another example of wrong detail, take what Vendler says about 'brag':

> When we say that the braggart brags . . . we mean that he intends to inform or remind us in his speech act of some of his real or imagined qualities, achievements, or possessions, with the added aim of provoking admiration or envy, which, in our [the speaker's] estimation, he does not deserve.[27]

The case of Muhammad Ali shows this description to be incorrect.[28] I can candidly and honestly remind you that Mu-

24. The use of this word may be changing (or may have recently changed). In my dialect, I don't believe it has a performative first person use (i.e., my dialect agrees with Vendler's description), but W. Follet (*Modern American Usage*, p. 57) cites a first person plural performative example, 'We allege that he had guilty knowledge'.

25. Recently the related adverb 'allegedly' has come to be attached to practically every public reference to crimes, evil-doings, immoralities, etc. Surely this use of this adverb is intended to connote *lack of proof (given)*, not *falsity*, of what was allegedly done.

26. Mathematicians often do, when the point is taken to be easily seen by the mathematically educated reader. Austin in *How to Do Things With Words* does this on p. 6; cf. also pp. 9–10, 13.

27. Vendler, "Illocutionary Suicide," p. 141.

28. I don't think Bobby Fischer would do equally well, since he doesn't seem to brag but just to *state* that he is the best chess player in the world —at least so he says, apparently quite sincerely.

hammad Ali, several years ago, was famous for bragging about
his own pugilistic qualities; he said he was "the greatest,"
meaning (I believe) the best professional heavyweight boxer.
At that time he *was* in fact "the greatest" in that sense and—
what would be held by many—he was deserving of admiration
and possibly[29] envy for being "the greatest." Since I don't
wish to dispute that he deserved admiration and there are
people who would assert that he did, how—referring to Vendler's
description—can I report that Muhammad Ali bragged about
being "the greatest"? Yet obviously I or any of us can report
this well-known fact, as I have just done.

Surely the moral point about bragging is that it is *itself* an
unseemly thing to do (modesty is a virtue)[30]—ordinarily. It is
just the last part of Vendler's description that is wrong, where
he says that the speaker who describes someone as bragging
means that that person does not deserve admiration or envy for
the things he boasts about. Sometimes people *do* deserve such
admiration, surely, and perhaps even envy; if they themselves
then voluntarily dwell on those admirable and enviable things,
they are bragging and can correctly and truly be said to be. If
Dr. Salk were to brag about discovering his vaccine, surely we
could report that he had bragged about it without implying that
that achievement didn't deserve our admiration. His bragging
would perhaps be unseemly; his achievement, however, was no
doubt thoroughly admirable and no doubt still is.

That is all the time I can spend on the details of Vendler's
descriptions. I repeat that the details are important in that they
furnish the test of his basic line of explanation of why quasi-
performatives are not genuine ones.

My other (and final) point is that there seem to be *other*
quasi-performative verbs than those dwelt on by Vendler which
even more clearly than those above cannot be accounted for by
his basic line. That is, there are other verbs that satisfy his
explanation (as revised) of what a quasi-performative is but
the report of which cannot plausibly be viewed as involving an
illocutionary aim a factor of which would have been spoiled in
the performative first person (if this use had existed for that
verb).

Vendler even refers to a couple of such verbs, though not
explicitly identifying them as quasi-performatives.[31] At one
point he says, "Blurting out a secret is distinct from, say, re-

29. It isn't clear to me that the notion of *deserving envy* really makes
sense, envy being a vice.
30. Cf. Vendler, "Illocutionary Suicide," p. 141, where he agrees.
31. I know of no place in his writings where either of them is classified.

vealing or betraying a secret." Consider then not the quasi-
performative 'blurt out' that he discusses but rather 'reveal':
as far as I can see, it too is a quasi-performative in Vendler's
sense, at least with a 'that'–clause complement. But it is a hard
case for his line, since (surely) there is no imputation of wrong-
doing or the like in its case—I mean none that is a built-in part
of its meaning or use.[32] It is simply that the thing revealed
is (a) interesting and (b) something that was not previously
known. But (a) and (b) provide no obstacle whatever to the
existence of a performative first person expression 'I (hereby)
reveal that p'; yet no such performative exists. Here, apparently,
is a quasi-performative, a verb like a performative except for not
having a performative first person use, *without* its report having
an illocutionary aim foiled by some performative first person
spoiling factor. I don't know *why* this sort of verb should exist,
but at any rate Vendler's basic line does not suffice to explain
why it should or, what is worse, how it *could*.

I would like now to bring into the discussion certain devices
that convert to a near-performative use many verbs that do not
themselves have a performative first person (as well as some that
do). The resulting verbal expressions might be termed *near-
performatives*, for they function in a very similar way and
satisfy analogues of Vendler's conditions,[33] although because
of their form they cannot satisfy all of those conditions (or
any of Austin's formulas) as they are originally stated. I refer
to verbal expressions of the forms

(8) (a) I will $V +$ e.g., 'I will move we
                                              adjourn' (thereby
                                              doing so)

     (b) I $\begin{cases} \text{'d} \\ \text{would} \end{cases} V +$ e.g., 'I would move
                                              the previous ques-
                                              tion (thereby
                                              doing so)

32. Not even, I think, as what Grice would call a "cancellable implication."

33. Near-performatives satisfy his conditions (a) and (b), i.e., they are
container-verbs of imperfect nominal complements; I think they satisfy
(c), human subject only, as well as performatives do. But they aren't of
course achievement verbs, since they are verbal constructions; as an
analogue of (d), which they satisfy, we might suggest (d'): that they are
such that saying one would V is an achievement in this sense (it is, namely,
to V). Similarly with (e): they occur in the first person singular, but 'will'
is future, not present, and I don't know what tense 'would' (or 'd') is
(note it is not the past tense meaning *used to*). 'Active' and 'noncontinuous' don't seem to make sense of these auxiliaries.

(c) I $\{$ 'd$\}$ like to $V +$ e.g., 'I'd like to
          $\{$would$\}$ reveal that p'
                                              (thereby doing so)

(d) I $\{$ 'd$\}$ like to try to $V +$ e.g., 'I'd like to try
          $\{$would$\}$ to convince you
                                              that p' (thereby
                                              trying to)

(e) May I $V + ?$ e.g., 'May I urge that
                                              we be careful
                                              about this matter?'
                                              (thereby so urging)

In (8), (a), (b), and (e) are probably uninteresting alternative ways of framing first person performatives (they seem less formal and/or more polite ways of doing so)[34] ; though performative verbs can be the V in them, perlocutionaries and quasi-performatives can't, when they have their performative-like force. But (c) provides near-performative utterances with a number of different V's: for example

(9) (i)   I'd like to suggest that your view may be mistaken
             (with an illocutionary V)
     (ii)   I'd like to persuade you of my sincerity in this
             matter
             (perlocutionary V)
     (iii) I'd like to brag a bit about my son's athletic
             prowess
             (Vendlerian quasi-performative V)
     (iv)   I'd like to reveal my daughter's approaching mar-
             riage
             (non-Vendlerian quasi-performative V)

The near-performative schema (8) (d) is (because of its 'try') fitted to take perlocutionary V's, as in

34. In fact, in my speech, the near-performative is often natural or possible when the performative hardly is—for example, 'I'd like to remark/note that p' is more natural for me than 'I remark/note that p' and I'm not sure I can say 'I welcome you' (though I can 'Welcome!', 'Welcome to our home!', and 'I'd like to welcome you to the colloquium'). 'I commiserate you in your loss' is very dubious, though 'I'd like to . . .', or better 'I want to . . .', is all right. At a recent meeting of the Faculty-Student Senate, I happened to notice one near-performative like (a) but with modal 'must', four examples of (b), and two of (c), all with performative V's (one was 'say'), as well as a couple of genuine performatives. (The meeting was rather informal in tone.)

(v) I'd like to try to convince you that my view is
   correct
          (perlocutionary *V*)

but it will also take some quasi-performatives, such as

(vi)   I'd like to try to goad this group into further study
      of these matters
          (quasi-performative *V*)

Note that these near-performative sentences also have other
meanings, as in 'I'd like to reveal my daughter's approaching
marriage, but unfortunately no one has asked her': 'like' seems
to have both this formulaic near-performative use and a straightforward descriptive (or avowal) use in which we say what we
(would) like. No doubt because of the modal auxiliary 'would',
these near-performatives do not, however, have a habitual-
present use[35] or a stage-direction-present use.

Returning to my final point about Vendler's basic line on
why quasi-performatives are quasi- rather than genuine, I want
now to try to improve that point by noting that some near-
performatives, such as (iii) above, involve quasi-performative
V's. If Vendler's explanation of why those quasi-performatives
(for example, 'brag') do not have a performative first person
use were correct, it would seem to suggest that an 'I'd like to
V' near-performative shouldn't exist either, which is contrary
to the facts in several cases.[36] In other cases the near-performative 'I'd like to try to *V*' exists for quasi-performative *V*'s, such
as (vi) above. It seems that Vendler's explanation would also
have the consequence that these did not exist, although they
do. But, to be just, suggesting that there *is* something right in
his explanation is the fact that 'egg on', 'goad', 'instigate', and
so on seem to have a weakened sense in those near-performatives,
as though to egg on, goad, instigate, or the like by using *this*
sort of utterance is a poor way of doing these things or a way
of doing them only in some secondary sense—even if not (as
Vendler's explanation would suggest) an impossible, conceptually incoherent way of doing them.

As a final note, let me mention one more class of verbs that
are candidates for quasi-performatives but also are such that
Vendler's basic line of explanation of their non-performative-

35. 'Would' of course has the *past*-tense habitual sense referred to in
note 33 above.
36. Thus, surely, in the cases of 'brag', 'boast', 'scold', 'nag', 'goad'
(cf. [vi] above), and 'incite', and possibly 'allege' and 'insinuate'.

ness would not work. These are certain verbs of *manner* of saying (as we might call them). Vendler suggests that none of these verbs takes indirect-discourse complements. Perhaps there is dialectal variation, but sentences like

(10) (i)   He murmured that he had to leave.
    (ii)   He shouted that he couldn't open the door.
    (iii) He gasped that he was having an asthma attack.

I personally find grammatically acceptable.[37] It seems to me that these verbs are achievement verbs, satisfying Vendler's condition (d); though murmuring, shouting, and gasping are "activities" (in Vendler's technical sense), what the sentences in (10) involve—murmuring, shouting, or gasping that *p*—seem to me to be "achievements". At any rate, they are not "accomplishments."[38] The other conditions, except for (e) (or [e″]), seem to be satisfied. As to (c), it applies to human subjects only; though a brook can murmur and many animals gasp (though not *shout*—they *cry* instead), they can't murmur or gasp (or shout) *that p*. I would assume that verbs of *manner* of saying are a subset of verbs of *saying*, or at least that verbs of manner of saying that take indirect-discourse complements are a subset of verbs of saying that take such complements.[39] So why aren't these verbs quasi-performatives? Or if they *are*, then what could possibly make them suicidal in the performative first person? One can murmur that someone murmured that *p*, shout that someone shouted that *p*, and even gasp that

37. They are quite as acceptable for me as their direct-discourse analogues

    (i′)   "I have to leave," he murmured.
    (ii′) "I can't open the door," he shouted.
    (iii′) "I'm having an asthma attack," he gasped.

I will add here that some verbs of manner of saying take both direct- and indirect-discourse complements (e.g., those just mentioned), some maybe only direct-discourse complements (e.g., I *think*, 'stutter'), but apparently none only *in*direct-discourse complements (as, say, 'believe' does)—unless certain quasi-performatives are verbs of manner of saying ('berate' might be a candidate), as dictionaries suggest.

38. These notions taken as they are defined in Vendler's "Verbs and Times," originally in *Philosophical Review,* 66 (1957): 143–60; reprinted in his *Linguistics in Philosophy* (Ithaca, N.Y.: Cornell University Press, 1967) as chap. 4. Roughly, to an *activity V*, the question 'How long did he *V*?' is appropriate; to an *accomplishment,* 'How long did it take him to *V*?'; to an *achievement* 'When (at what moment) did he *V*?'.

39. They are, according to the definition I gave as (7) above.

someone gasped that *p;* but still instances of the sentence-schemata

(11) (i)   I murmur that *p*.
     (ii) I shout that *p*.
     (iii) I gasp that *p*.

have only the habitual-present and stage-direction-present uses. I don't know what the explanation of this is, but Vendler's basic line again seems inadequate to explain why this is so or even how it could be.[40]

There are points of detail in Vendler's particular descriptions of the use of his examples of quasi-performatives that relate to his basic line that I disagree with and that I will close by not discussing.

40. I would like to acknowledge the help of my colleague Richard Faber in seeing the relevance of this last class of verbs to Vendler's views on quasi-performatives. He also raised for me the interesting case of 'explain'. The remarks made about 'murmur', etc., seem also to apply to it, when it is completed with a 'that'–clause. At a certain time and without preliminary activity, one just explains that *p*. But one can explain a theory, for example, or how one got into philosophy in the first place for hours on end, and this without one's doing so necessarily culminating in a "climax" (as Vendler puts it in "Verbs and Times"); explaining *wh*-seems to be an activity, rather than an achievement. Yet if I explain *that* I got into philosophy by mistake, then surely I have explained *how* I got into philosophy (or have I only purported to?); and, conversely, can I explain *how* I got into philosophy without explaining that *p*, for some *p* or other, such as that I got into it by mistake? It would seem not. Are different meanings of 'explain' involved in the two cases? I incline to think not. Then what *is* explaining, an activity or an achievement? And if it is the latter (or is in one sense the latter), isn't it a quasi-performative? Perhaps here one must also take condition (c), human subjects only, as a necessary condition.

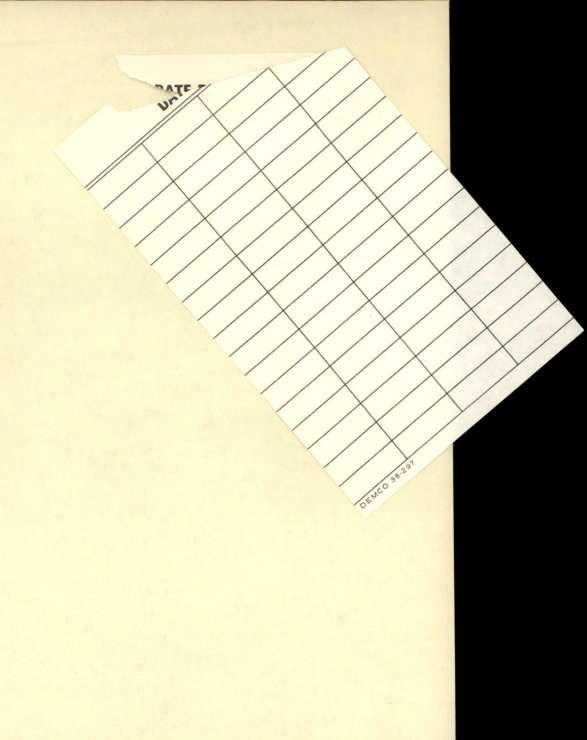

DATE

DEMCO 38-297